Grappa

Grappa

A GUIDE TO THE BEST

AXEL *and* BIBIANA BEHRENDT

Photographs by Bodo A. Schieren

ABBEVILLE PRESS PUBLISHERS

NEW YORK LONDON PARIS

Translated from the German by Russell Stockman

ENGLISH-LANGUAGE EDITION
Editor: Nancy Grubb
Designer: Patricia Fabricant
Production Editor: Kerrie Baldwin
Production Manager: Louise Kurtz

First published in the United States of America in 2000 by Abbeville Press, 22 Cortlandt Street, New York, N.Y. 10007.

Copyright 1999 by Wilhelm Heyne Verlag GmbH & Co. KG, Munich (tenth printing, enlarged and updated). English translation copyright © 2000 Abbeville Press.

Library of Congress Catalog Card Number 99-89628

CONTENTS

PREFACE

———◄○►———

*F*orget the throat-burning grappa that the pizzeria owner down the block used to offer you after your meal. This once-cheap after-dinner tipple has changed—in style, in quality, and in status. Not since Scotch whisky conquered the world a century ago has a spirit managed to establish itself so strongly on the international market. And grappa is no passing fad. In the past ten or twenty years it has been admitted into the exclusive club of recognized classics, with the most exquisite cognacs, the noblest malt whiskies, and the most delicate fruit brandies. It doesn't take a market wizard to recognize that this is an irreversible trend.

Although the grappa phenomenon is relatively recent, the array of Italian pomace brandies has grown so rapidly in the last few years that it is now almost impossible to survey completely; more and more distilleries are producing more and more grappa variants, and in these boom times nearly every winegrower has also begun distilling his own grappa or having it distilled for him. No one can say how many different grappas are now available, but they doubtless number in the thousands, and at least a few hundred of them are exported.

It was therefore high time that somebody attempted to provide an overview, sort through the available products, evaluate them, and create out of this giant puzzle a distinct picture—even if only a snapshot, a subjective impression.

Which brands and varieties were to be included? We consulted friends, colleagues, connoisseurs, vintners, importers, associations, international experts and gastronomes, and our own personal tastes. At last we settled on a hundred or so producers with their various grappas—a mix of big names and lesser-known discoveries. No such selection can be "correct." Many a grappa fan will find that his own favorite, discovered who knows when or where, is not included. That is lamentable but could not be avoided. A person's passion for a favorite grappa can be unbounded, but a book can have only a finite number of pages.

Needless to say, we assume full responsibility for any injustices in our selection of vintners and distilleries—and would be grateful for constructive criticism, tips, suggestions of any kind. We will gladly consider including them in any future editions. We would like to thank here all of the people who helped us in our research, but to name them all would require space that is—again—not available.

It has already been five years since the first edition of this guide was published in Germany (this is its first appearance in English). In the interim there has been much discussion and—in the absence of reliable market data—much speculation about the grappa boom. Some forecasters feel that the grappa market will continue to expand unchecked; others, that it will ultimately level off; and still others, that it will decline and prove to have been only a temporary fashion. It is our impression that the trend will continue unbroken, especially the trend toward better and better quality.

It is apparent that sales of high-priced grappas continue to increase out of all proportion to the liquor market as a whole, often by as much as 20 to 30 percent a year. In this updated edition we have tried to do justice to this phenomenon by including even more top producers. We wish our readers pleasant tasting.

The Long Road to Fame

—◦—

*G*rappa's phenomenal success may be quite recent, but its roots extend deep into the past. Just how deep is suggested by its name. The root of the word may come from the Middle Latin *rapus,* for grape. In the vulgar Latin of Northern Italy one finds the terms *ràspòn, rapo, gràpo, rappe, ràspe,* or even *graspa,* an old term for pomace that is still used by many producers today.

There are several contradictory theories about the origin of grappa. Some historians maintain that it was the Burgundians who brought the art of distilling to Friuli at the beginning of the fifth century. Others insist that the Friulians knew the technique even earlier. Still others place the birth of grappa in the ninth century, when Sicily was occupied by the Arabs—a connection that is perhaps not so far-fetched, for it was the Arabs who discovered distilling and introduced it to Europe. (The word *alcohol,* for example, comes from the Arabic *al khôl.*)

But just when and where the first drop of grappa dripped from some primitive distilling apparatus lies hidden in the mists of history. Suffice it to say that grappa is roughly fifteen hundred years old—gallantry demands that one not try to pin down the age of such a venerable dame more precisely.

Even though there are no definite records concerning its beginnings, early documents include frequent mention of grappa. A will dated 1451 includes among the goods to be bequeathed a cellar full of strong spirits as well as a device for making aquavit *(unum ferrum ad faciendam acquavitem)*—identified later in the same document as *"grape."* The heirs were doubtless delighted, for in the fifteenth century there was already brisk commerce in grappa, including export to various European countries. Production was licensed, and even then various taxes were levied on distillates from both wine and pomaces.

Illegal trade in spirits is as old as the art of distilling. To prevent widespread smuggling, peasants were permitted to distill grappa for their own use—a welcome concession at a time when lords were paid their tithes in wine and a vintner was rarely left with anything more than the pressed pomace. It is only logical that grappa, even though a comfort for many after a hard day's work, was long considered just a poor people's drink. Winegrowers and other farmers passed down their secrets for making grappa from one generation to the next, refining their processes over the centuries. It seemed that grappa would always remain in the shadows.

It was only in our own century—more precisely, beginning in the 1960s and '70s—that grappa became caught up in the revolution of the world of spirits. An elegant Italian cuisine had been developed, making culinary waves both in Europe and beyond and achieving international acclaim equivalent to that long enjoyed by the cooking of France. Italian wines had gained new respect as well, as winegrowers either turned to the grape varieties internationally desired or revived ancient, nearly forgotten traditional ones. They revised their methods with an eye toward quality from the vineyard to the cellar, and as a result more and more of their vintages were attaining world-class stature.

Given the circumstances, the rediscovery of grappa was virtually inevitable. Pomace brandies concentrated the aromas and specific qualities of the improved vintages and constituted the final touch in a culture of elegant dining and drinking. A handful of distillers and winegrowers saw its potential, and with their pioneer labors they unleashed a veritable grappa boom. They devised and tested new techniques, experimented with single-variety pomaces and unusual production methods, and called attention to their products with creative packaging. The crude, rustic, thick-walled grappa bottle was transformed into a fragile, handblown crystal carafe of Murano glass—in fact, a whole glass menagerie of different colors and shapes. These innovators felt that it was just as important to delight the eye as it was to titillate the palate.

They were right. The onetime peasant drink attracted the gaze of gastronomes and epicures now that it was done up like a top model in a chic new outfit. Modern design can work miracles, but one often wishes that the same degree of care had been taken with the contents as with the packaging.

It must be said, however, that grappa owes its triumphant career as much to its adoring fans as to its professional handlers. It first conquered the top Italian restaurants around the world. Carts of after-dinner drinks came to be stocked with more and more eye-catching and more and more expensive grappa varieties. After all, who cares about expense when tempted by such attractive aids to digestion? Eventually, a simple peasant drink became high fashion, then a trend became a boom and a cultural artifact turned into a cult object.

Like any cult, that of grappa has spawned its bizarre off-shoots—excesses and exaggerations of a trend that in itself is all

"Easter Grappa," by Ernesto Barozzi

to the good. Take, for example, the Easter grappa created by Ernesto Barozzi. His idea: nest foil-wrapped chocolate eggs in the hollow at the bottom of the bottle. Pretty, to be sure, but not necessarily appealing after a big Easter dinner.

What creativity in the truest sense of the word can produce is demonstrated by Antonella Bocchino. The grappa-obsessed daughter of the Bocchino family concern distills not only grapes, pomaces, and fruits but also flowers, even orchids that she has flown in from Japan. There's nothing wrong with new olfactory experiences, however far-fetched. And we certainly have no quarrel with the houses of Barozzi and Bocchino, both of which distill outstanding grappas. But even though creativity and experimentation deserve respect, a local product as firmly established as grappa shouldn't have to put on airs.

Another prime example of the degree to which the cult of grappa can succumb to excesses is the glorification of the Piedmont's Romano Levi. Although he is unquestionably one of the pioneers if not the founder of the grappa craze, we ultimately decided not to include him in the main section of this book. We thought about it, long and hard. Levi is myth and hermit in one—

Antonella Bocchino even distills flowers

an eccentric, if you will, who has been distilling with antiquated equipment since 1945, and whose highly traditional grappas have very little in common with the successful modern ones.

So far so good. But it is precisely the quality of Levi grappas that is debatable. One frequently hears that his distillates are impure, that they taste scorched or like rubber. And it is true that his grappas occasionally "flunk" in blind tastings or are simply removed from competition. That does not alter the fact that retailers occasionally ask astronomical prices for them—something for which Levi himself is hardly to blame. His limited output is sold not so much on the market as under the counter; those who want some of it are lucky to turn up the odd bottle. Early producers like Levi have become big business—but not always legal business, as evidenced by the illustration on the next page of confiscated forgeries of Levi's bottles. Forgers do have a nose for what's hot.

For our part, we found that we could not do justice to the much-debated Levi myth. His adherents may take comfort from the fact that even though he is not included in our alphabetical listing—precisely because he is such a special case—we have at

Romano Levi, a living legend

least mentioned him prominently here, thereby acknowledging his lifetime achievement.

Romano Levi is a living legend, a symbol of the extraordinary stature now accorded to grappa. Whether the grappa boom has already passed its peak or not yet even approached it we will have to patiently wait and see—while taking pleasure in tasting the best of the brands available.

Confiscated fake
Levi grappas

Grappa: A Definition

*L*ike its siblings, France's marc and Germany's Tresterbrand, grappa is a pomace brandy produced by direct distillation of the skins of pressed grapes. Yet grappa, for all its similarity to its siblings, has a wholly different character. Even its name is exclusive: only distillates produced in Italy can be marketed as "grappa." This historic right is recognized by the European Union and established by law.

To keep its taste as unmistakable as its name, every aspect of grappa's production is prescribed by statute: the composition of the pomace (the skins, seeds, and so on left after the grapes are crushed for wine), the distillation method, and the maximum alcohol content (86 percent by volume) of the fresh distillate. Even the maximum moisture content of the pomace has been fixed. Distillates from whole fermented grapes, though similar in taste, cannot be called "grappa." These have been given their own name: acquavite d'uva.

Both grappas and acquavite d'uva are made by direct distillation. This is simple in the case of acquavite d'uva, for which the raw material is grape must (juice), but producing grappa requires great skill, for it is difficult to distill a solid. Because adding water to the pomace is prohibited, elaborate preparation and preservation of the pomace and expensive distilling methods are required. If distillation is successful, the grappa will present a fullness of flavors not generally achieved by the purer, less potent acquavite d'uva. This wealth of aroma is preserved only if the alcohol content is less than the maximum allowed: the lower the alcohol level of the fresh distillate the more intense and complex the flavor.

From Grape to Pomace:
Taste Is No Accident

◄○►

$\mathcal{T}$he same laws apply for all producers, whether vintners or distilleries, and at first glance their techniques do not appear to be so very dissimilar, yet their grappas are extremely different, encompassing a whole world of varied aromas. To understand how a grappa gets its distinctive taste, it is necessary to look at its origins in wine and winegrowing.

Despite the very great differences between grappa and conventional brandies distilled from wine, grappa is also ultimately a product of the vineyard, of the ripening grape on the vine. The quality of the soil, the vine variety, the vineyard's microclimate, and the weather are as important for a grappa as they are for a

Chardonnay, the trendy grape of the moment

wine. Moreover, the vintner's "style," his approach to winegrowing and his treatment of his vines, his decisions with respect to harvesting and fermenting, all have a direct effect on grappa's raw material, the pomace. All of these determine the quality of the final distillate, affect its aroma, give it its character, even its idiosyncracies.

GRAPE VARIETIES

In response to the devastating scourge of phylloxera in the last century, which spared virtually no major winegrowing region, countless new grape varieties were developed in Europe and abroad, traditional ones were varied by hybridization, and the winegrower's choices greatly expanded. Moves toward liberalization and partial standardization following the formation of the European Union have added still more. New plantings of foreign strains have joined each region's indigenous varieties, developed over the centuries through mutations of the original vines. Experimentation and the desire to adapt to current fashions have meant that in the heartlands of Italy's grappa culture—in Friuli, the Veneto, and the Piedmont—many plantings of traditional vine varieties have given way to the current favorites chardonnay, sauvignon blanc, cabernet sauvignon, and pinot noir. Naturally this has left its mark on the regions' grappas.

Some grape varieties are better suited for the production of grappa than others in that they have a higher concentration of aromatic substances—aromas that are passed on to the wine and also to the distillate, giving them greater character in smell and taste. Among the more ideal ones are Riesling, Müller-Thurgau, gewürztraminer, and muscat. With practice it is possible to recognize the grape variety by its special taste, especially in the distillates from its pomaces.

Other grape varieties tend to pass along a rather neutral aroma that is scarcely noticeable in the distillate. Grappas from such varieties are not necessarily of lesser quality; their bouquet and their flavor will still exhibit the typical character of a pomace brandy. But since winegrowers and distillers of single-variety grappas proudly identify that variety on their labels, buyers naturally expect to taste echoes of the given grape—and are frequently disappointed. Grappas made from chardonnay, for example, often fail to exhibit the expected qualities. It is our experience that red wine pomaces generally tend to be best for distilling—for good reason, as we will explain below.

HARVESTING

By his choice of grape varieties the winegrower can influence the ratio of acid content to must weight, a factor crucial to the quality of the resulting pomace distillate. But he can also have a very dramatic influence by choosing when to harvest so as to achieve the desired character in his wine. Unfortunately, that may not be the ideal time to harvest with respect to grappa, which benefits from a higher acid content (the earlier the harvest, the more acidic the grape). The pomace from a premier wine does not necessarily produce a distinguished grappa.

CLIMATE

Climate is another important factor in determining the quality of a grappa. The warmer the region and the more sunlight it receives, the more rapidly the acid in the grapes decomposes, resulting in an inferior distillate. For this reason, grappas from the cooler regions of the north tend to be more complex and elegant than the hearty distillates of the south. It is no coincidence that the recent grappa phenomenon originated in the winegrowing regions of northern Italy, in the shelter of the Alps. Even so, many Tuscan, Umbrian, even Sicilian grappas are among the very best available. The microclimate of the specific vineyard plays an important role, and in combination with other factors it can produce pleasant surprises.

Limiting Quantity

Bulk Italian wines finally appear to be a thing of the past. Reduced per capita consumption of wine as a result of the new health consciousness and overproduction all over Europe have led to drastic price reductions, causing winegrowers to revise their strategies. Even the odd wine scandal has had a positive effect. Today the Italians are producing much less wine but wine of superior quality. Smaller quantities assure more extracts and greater fullness. Reduced per-acre yields have definitely enhanced the aromatic content of each individual grape, which benefits the pomace and with it the resulting grappa.

The Pomace

In wine making, the solid residue that is left after pressing is referred to as the pomace, or marc. Traditionally it included stems, stalks, and seeds as well as skins. But vintners determined to produce smooth, high-quality wines now remove the stems before pressing, thereby preventing their bitter substances from flavoring the must. Nowadays the stems are also removed if the pomace is to be distilled, because otherwise the distillery will refuse to accept it.

On delivery, the raw material from which a fine distillate is created is nothing more than a wagonload of grape pulp smelling sweetly of must. In recent years its moisture content has noticeably increased, for the grapes are no longer pressed to the last drop as they were in the days of mass production. This is another way in which the reduced emphasis on quantity has led to higher quality; the transfer of bitter substances to the must has been minimized. Richly aromatic, the resulting pomaces make good grappas.

Pressing and Fermentation

Although grappa has taken its place among the noblest and most expensive spirits, as a pomace distillate it is essentially only a by-product of wine making. It is the vintner who determines the condition of the pomace after pressing and fermentation. How long the mash is fermented, leaving the pomace in contact with the must, depends on the grape variety and the type of wine desired. To produce a fresh, lively white wine, for example, it is necessary to press the grapes immediately so that a minimum amount of tannin is released from the skins and the fruity acids are kept as pure as possible. Making a durable red wine with deep color is a wholly different process. In this case the tannins and dyes from the skins are essential, and are extracted through long fermentation of the mash.

Pomaces awaiting further processing in the distillery

When delivered to the distillery, pomaces are therefore in all different stages of fermentation, and the degree of fermentation directly influences the quality and taste of the distillate. Distillers distinguish between three main kinds of pomace: pure, half-fermented, and fully fermented.

Pure, unfermented pomaces are provided mainly by makers of white wines. They must be fermented before they are distilled, which is a tricky matter. It is possible to add a little yeast to foster fermentation, but the quantity is strictly regulated and there is always the danger of unwanted fermentations. Moreover, the longer the pomace is left standing the more moisture it loses, moisture that cannot be replaced.

Half-fermented pomaces are generally what is left from the production of rosato, or Italian rosé. Brief fermentation of the mash releases a small amount of color from the skins but preserves a certain freshness in the finished wine. In this case the pomace manages to absorb aromatic components from the must, and the ultimate distillate therefore has a more intense flavor than one made from white wine pressings. These pomaces must also be fermented before distilling in order to transform the remaining sugars into alcohol; however, the risk to the distiller is considerably reduced by the shorter standing time.

Most grappas are made from fermented pomaces resulting from the production of red wine. Having been left in the mash until fermentation is complete, such pomaces have been enriched through long contact with the must and its aromatic yeast products and can be distilled immediately. This is why grappas made from red wine pomaces tend to be purest and have the greatest character.

The Art of Distilling

———◦►———

Once the wine maker has completed his fermentation and pressing and delivered his pomace to the distillery, everything must proceed very quickly. To produce a good grappa it is necessary to ensure that virtually no air reaches the pomace, for air can only bring problems—and possibly even a touch of vinegar, which could render the pomace unusable.

DISTILLING TECHNIQUES

The fruit sugar in the grapes is transformed into high-percentage alcohol in two steps. It begins during the harvest: the pressure of their own weight is enough to make the grapes burst open before they are out of the vineyard. The grape juice thus comes in contact with the skin of the fruit, with its clinging microorganisms and yeasts. Uncontrolled fermentation begins as the grape sugar is attacked by the grape yeast and transformed into alcohol and volatile carbon dioxide. Pressing hastens the process, and the end product is a wine with a maximum alcohol content of roughly 15 percent by volume.

A second stage—distillation—is required to derive high-percentage alcohol from the remaining pomace. Owing to the different boiling points of the various components, it is possible to separate the alcohol from water and undesirable fusel oils. The pomace is heated until it gives off steam, which is then captured, cooled, and condensed into a liquid. The highly volatile substances such as methyl alcohol, ethyl esters of acetic acid, and acetaldehyde have the lowest boiling point, and since they not only ruin the taste of the distillate but are in some cases poisonous, they are cut off from the run as the so-called head. The purest alcohol and aromatic substances appear as steam at medium temperatures. Only this middle part of the run, the "heart" of the distillation, is condensed into grappa. In the "tail," which is also cut off, are water and still more impurities, chiefly fusel oils such as amyl alcohol. The distiller has to be able to distinguish between the several phases and be certain of capturing only the middle run. The more successfully it is separated from the head and tail, the purer and more delicate the distillate.

Distilling pomace is a difficult business. The fermented leftovers after pressing have a low alcohol content and a high percentage of impurities. In successive distillations, also called rectification, the brandy is further purified. A disgorging device built into the system constantly returns "phlegmatic" components (those not so readily vaporized) to the still, where they are reheated and a higher yield of aromatics and alcohol is obtained.

Discontinuous Distilling

The origins of alcohol distilling are obscure, but even though we know nothing specific about the method first employed, it must have been in principle the same that is used today: a fermented

Modern technology for classic distillates. In addition to the increasingly important wine makers' grappas, countless top brands are produced in large quantities in mechanized distilleries. Even here, however, the single-batch, or discontinuous, method is generally used in order to obtain brandies with the greatest character and individuality.

liquid is heated in a vessel, and the rising vapors are captured, drawn off, and condensed by cooling into a liquid with a higher alcohol content. Simple and inexpensive to operate, the still, or alembic, is a device used all over the world, whether in the production of cognac or Armagnac, malt whisky or rum. No distillery could function without it.

But it also has its disadvantages. After each batch the vessel must be cleaned and refilled, so repeated distilling is both time-consuming and laborious. Distilling grappa presents yet another problem. The application of heat to the bottom of the still tends to quickly scorch the solid mass of the pomace even if water is added, resulting in unwanted aromas. In this context, it is worth noting that Italian legislation relating to the production of spirits (No. 1559 of December 7, 1951) requires "that distillation be accomplished in such a way as to avoid any unpleasant taste." A simple technical refinement made this possible: a double-walled vessel with circulating water in the space between the walls, called a double-bottomed pot still. With such a vessel the heat is less intense and distributed evenly around the pomace.

Such stills are expensive, and operating them takes a long time, so this method has not been adopted too widely. Nevertheless, a number of distillers in the Piedmont, the Trentino, and the Alto Adige prefer this water-filled alembic. They see the long time required as a plus, as it allows them to separate with great precision the heart of the run from the undesired substances. For this reason, the words *distillata a bagnomaria* (distilled in a water bath) on a label are definitely an indication of quality.

Another invention, the steam alembic, has had more success. One occasionally sees it referred to on labels as well: *distillata a vapore.* Invented during the second half of the last century, this steam technique is used by distillers who want to preserve the individual character of their product but who also want to operate economically and without the aroma risks of other methods. They place the pomace inside the vessel either on a perforated insert or on bundles of twigs. This prevents the damp mass from cooking and solidifying, making it easier to clean the vessel once the process is completed. Steam is forced through the pomace from below, causing the alcohol to evaporate and releasing its volatile aromatics. A device called a *colonna,* or column, attached to the vessel, is normally used to cut off the head and tail of the run. Steam collected on its perforated plates is condensed into different cooling vessels, effectively separating pure grappa from unwanted impurities.

CONTINUOUS DISTILLING

In the mid-1960s traditional distilling in pot stills fell somewhat out of style. An apparatus developed in the United States especially for solid substances like pomace made the production of grappa not only simpler and faster but also less expensive.

The technique of continuous distilling had been invented a century before, revolutionizing the production of many traditional spirits and ensuring purer, lighter-tasting distillates of uniform quality. It made possible the production of blended whiskies in Scotland, changed the character of Irish whiskey, created a boom in light, white rum, and in general forced local, handmade brandies off the market in favor of industrially produced brands. But that technique worked only for liquids, whereas pomace, being solid, still had to be distilled in the old way. In the new method small batches of pomace are fed by conveyor into a prewarming chamber before they reach the actual still. There they are heated with steam and the spent pomace is automatically ejected. A complex system of heating and cooling columns assures that the heart is expertly separated from the head and tail of the run and that the distillate is of uniform quality.

Aging

——◦►——

Like fruit brandies, grappas have a special, highly pleasant character the moment they are distilled. Unlike rum or whiskey, they do not require long aging to attain maturity and harmony or to fully develop their aroma.

Six months' aging is required by law, and this is assured by storage in bond. Owing to the booming demand for grappa over the past few years and the undisputed quality and distinct flavor of even young grappas, most of what reaches the market is "white" or young grappa.

A number of distillers nevertheless give their grappa a longer period in the barrel, allowing it to incorporate tannins from the wood and to acquire a much fuller, more rounded body. Once the distillate has aged at least six months in the barrel and an additional six months in airtight glass flasks or stainless-steel tanks, the designations *invecchiata* (aged), *stravecchia* (very old), or *riserva* (reserve) can be added to the label. These are not always a guarantee of exquisite flavor: the fresh character of a grappa can be overwhelmed by too strong wood notes and end up tasting like an old brandy.

Developing a grappa in the barrel is a tricky process. The natural aromatic fullness of many grappas calls for delicate treatment. One has to choose the right wood for the barrel since its tannins and aromatics will flavor the distillate. It is essential that the distillate attain finesse and delicacy without being overwhelmed.

Italy's centuries-old tradition of aging wine in wood barrels provided a certain fund of knowledge. But aging grappa in barrels has a long history as well; studies of how various woods affect the distillate were done in the nineteenth century. An aged grappa was considered a synonym for quality as well as a status symbol at a time when only the wealthy could afford to keep large stores of comestibles on hand for long periods. Reports from that era recommend Polish oak from the woods around Gdansk and Szczecin; French oak from the Limousin, the Troncais, or Nièvre; Yugoslav oak; and Italian ash, cherry, or mulberry. Chestnut was not advised, for it colored the distillate too deeply, making it appear to be impure.

In the twentieth century, wood aging was standardized, and grappa is now consistently aged in large casks made of Slovenian oak. The only question has been their capacity, which can vary from 2,000 to 10,000 liters (about 528 to 2,640 gallons). Improved coopering techniques saw to it that the barrels allowed very little oxygen to reach the distillate and that the brandy was tempered evenly, without taking on too many undesirable flavors. Once uniform aging was possible, grappas became both softer and sweeter while retaining their unique character.

It was only in the late 1960s that distillers began experimenting with other types of barrels. In the wake of the *barrique* craze in wine making, small barrels made of French oak varieties came into vogue and people began to clamor for the "Limousin tone," the "Allier note," or the "Troncais aroma." At this same time, limited quantities of top-quality grappa were aged in small to tiny casks of pearwood, applewood, almond wood, cherry, or mulberry—and occasionally even juniper. Each different wood contributes its own distinctive aromatic components to the distillate: oak, for example, is perceived as tart, cherry as somewhat sweetish. Such experiments were not without their critics, who claimed that the wood notes only masked aroma flaws or changed the grappa's character without improving it.

Flavored Grappas

Grappas can take on additional flavor components not only from the barrel but also from the addition of herbs. Like many other spirits, grappa served as the basis for any number of herbal tonics in centuries past, before the rise of modern medicines.

The flavored grappas of today have virtually nothing in common with those "home remedies." Devotees of the former treasure the variety of flavors that can be achieved by the addition of herbal extracts or fruits. Whether added in their fresh state or as alcoholic extracts, all such flavorings are permitted by law so long as they are natural in origin. Especially popular is *grappa alla ruta,* a grappa to which sprigs of rue have been added. Other aromatics are juniper, caraway, anise, cloves, mint, cinnamon, cinchona (quinine), almonds, pine nuts, cinnamon, lemon balm, and rhubarb. Bilberry, strawberry, and raspberry grappas are quite popular in Italy.

Interesting as the addition of aromatics may be as a change, they rob the grappa of some of its original character as a grape distillate, and for that reason we have chosen not to include flavored grappas in our catalog section. Wine is the very soul of grappa, and a wine is always a reflection of its homeland, the product of a specific landscape.

Barrel aging gives the distillate color, roundness, and additional aromas.

Winegrowing Regions

———◦►———

*L*ike virtually no other distillate, grappa captures and re-fines the aroma and taste of the substance from which it is made. Vintner grappas, especially, reflect the winegrowing region in which they were produced. The following is a brief overview of the regions covered in this book, proceeding from north to south, west to east.

PIEDMONT

The Piedmont is one of Italy's most important winegrowing regions. Centuries of experience in producing top international wines and the efforts of innovative vintners have assured the landscape a prominent place in the world's wine atlas.

It is also a culinary landscape: one thinks of the famous white truffles from the extensive oak forests in the vicinity of Alba, of an abundance of berries and herbs. Mushrooms of all kinds thrive in woods flanked by well-tended vineyards, especially the strong-smelling *Boletus edulus*—harbingers of autumn whose characteristic aromatic notes are imparted to Piedmont wines as well. Even neighboring Frenchmen praise these wines for their spicy fullness.

The best Piedmont vineyards are on the slopes of the Monferrato range east of Turin, the vermouth capital. The microclimate in the lee of this mighty massif and the hot, windless summers ensure a long growing season, one that gives strength to the vines and body to the finished wine. Mist blows up from the sea in the fall, spreading fog across the many bodies of water in this fertile region and imparting a tart freshness to the sub-alpine climate—the ideal conditions for tannin-rich, muscular wines.

The worldwide reputation of the Piedmont's vintages was established not too many years ago by its red wine—in good years equal to the best wines of France and deliberately crafted to resemble them in taste. Its barolo, the luscious red wine from the nebbiolo grape, is superb once it has been aged.

Other Piedmont wines have found recognition as well. These may not compete with barolo but they do have virtues of their own: the light barbaresco, for example, produced in Neive, Treiso, and the town from which it takes its name; the dark Barbera d'Asti, d'Alba, or del Monferrato; the slightly sparkling Brachetto d'Acqui; the Grignolino from Asti or Monferrato Casalese. Not to forget the red dolcetto, the best of which, from Alba, is known for its soft, youthful tone. The region also produces white wines that have sparked international trends: the cortese or Gavi di Gavi, produced in the villages Gavi, Carrosio, Bosio, and Parodi in the province of Alessandria. There is also the Moscato d'Asti, a muscat wine from the provinces Asti, Cuneo, and Alessandria that is the basis for the aromatic sparkling wine Asti Spumante and is also popular as a dessert wine. In the last few years, study of the region's long winegrowing tradition

The Piedmont in autumn, time of the grape harvest

has led to the rediscovery and increased cultivation of native Piedmont vine varieties: timorasso, bonarda, pelaverga, ruché, and many others—long forgotten strains nearly threatened with extinction. Some of these are documented as typical vines of the region as early as the thirteenth century. In addition, a number of the international trendsetters have been added in recent decades—burgundy vines like pinot blanc, pinot gris, pinot noir, and chardonnay, as well as the sauvignon siblings cabernet and sauvignon blanc.

This combination of tradition and innovation has also led to the production of classic and modern variants of the rediscovered peasant-style grappa. In a wine landscape as varied as the Piedmont, all manner of finds can be made among pomace distillates as well.

TRENTINO–ALTO ADIGE (SOUTH TYROL)

The north Italian wine regions of the Trentino and Alto Adige extend along the valley of the Adige. Driving into Italy across the Brenner Pass, one first reaches the Alto Adige—or South Tyrol—with its wine and spa town Merano. In the Y-shaped growing

Along the upper course of the Adige

area along the Adige and the Isarco, vineyards are grouped around the provincial capital Bolzano (Bozen) and its neighboring communities St. Magdalena, Terlan, and Caldaro, and follow the river southward into the Trentino, which begins at Mezzocorona and ends to the north of Lake Garda.

Although nearly 80 percent of the region's production consists of red wines—notably the light vernaccio from the Lago di Caldaro and the Colli di Bolzano—the Alto Adige, with altitudes over three thousand feet (915 meters) in the Cembra Valley and a mild, sunny climate, is also ideally suited for the production of white wines with bite and character. The region's wines made from Riesling and sylvaner grapes, the gewürztraminer from Termeno, and its sauvignons and white pinots have enjoyed world-class stature for some time, something its red wines have attained only recently.

The Trentino is also red wine country; 85 percent of its production is made up of reds and rosés, most of them agreeable everyday wines. By reducing yields, crafting sophisticated *cuvées,* and aging in *barriques* (small oak barrels), the area's wine-growers have also managed to create over the past twenty-five years a number of first-class, highly distinctive wines that are internationally acclaimed.

In the Alto Adige as in the Trentino, the revolutions of the last few years have changed the face of the wine landscape. Native vine varieties like lagrein, schiava, nosiola, traminer, and gold and rosé muscat had given way to the more modern vines chardonnay, sauvignon, cabernet, and merlot, but more recently a certain balance between region-specific and internationally fashionable varieties has been achieved.

VENETO

Venice's historical hinterland, its Terra Ferma, extends to Lake Garda in the west, to the foothills of the Dolomites in the north, and to the plain of the Po and Emilia-Romagna in the south.

Its geographical boundaries may be firmly fixed, but the

Veneto has broken through the limits of Italy's winegrowing tradition more consistently than anywhere else. The famous red wines of Bordeaux have found a second home here; the region's cabernets and merlots, cultivated in the Bordelais manner, have long since ceased to be mere imitations and have become some of the highest-rated products in the world of wine.

Even in Verona, the center of the production of soave, valpolicella, and bardolino, vintners are moving with the times: the annual wine fair VinItaly, which is held in this "wine capital of Italy," serves as a showcase for the newest developments in the Italian wine business.

The Breganze region, farther to the north, has made a name for itself in the last few years with its red merlots and cabernets as well as its white pinot grigios. Its native vine varieties vespaiolo, freisa, and gropello are now of virtually no importance.

For a few years now the sparkling wine called prosecco for short, after its vine variety, has become the vogue worldwide. It comes from the Conegliano region in the northern Veneto, at the foot of the Dolomites. The best proseccos come from the village of Valdobbiadene and carry the site designation Cartizze.

FRIULI–VENEZIA GIULIA

The region known as Friuli–Venezia Giulia extends roughly sixty-five miles (104 kilometers) westward from the Slovenian border near Trieste toward Venice. Despite its peripheral location, it is one of the most important producers of quality wines in Italy. In part this is because it has a winegrowing tradition reaching back thousands of years; its reputation already made by the time of Julius Caesar, it became a prized conquest for the Roman empire. Its ancient port city of Aquileia was the chief transfer point for the Roman wine trade with Germany and northern Europe. Friuli owes its great variety of vines to frequent changes of rule between the Hapsburgs, the Venetians, and the French, and also to its ability to impose clear and consistent labeling; since there had been no continuity, no traditions had developed to stand in the way of the new regulations. Neatly divided into six DOC *(denominazione di origine controllata)* regions, Friuli now cultivates more than a dozen vine varieties; its native verduzzo, schioppettino, refosco, tocai friuliano, ribbola gialla, pignolo, tacelenghe, and the rare picolit are all making a comeback.

TUSCANY

The vineyards, olive groves, and architecture of this central Italian region blend to create an almost ideal landscape. Its most important wine is Chianti: Chianti Classico is produced in the traditional heartland between Florence and Siena; ordinary Chianti, from the four vine varieties sangiovese, canaiolo, trebbiano, and malvasia in six additional areas. For some time now the addition of small percentages of other varieties, among them cabernet and merlot, has been permitted. Other top-quality wines are Brunello di Montalcino and Vino Nobile di Montepulciano. Superb whites are Montecarlo Bianco and Vernaccia di San Gimignano—as the first Tuscan white wine, the latter was granted the designation DOCG *(denominazione di origine controllata e garantita)* as

Tuscany, a blend of landscape and architecture

proof of guaranteed quality. All these wines enjoyed a high reputation for centuries, but they lost much of their stature in the first two-thirds of the twentieth century. This was largely due to mass production, which resulted in both red and white wines being sold for pennies in the huge straw-covered bottles called *fiaschi*. The decline led the region's vintners to rethink their positions. Stricter rules were imposed for DOC wines, and there was a radical push toward quality. More and more producers studied wine making in France, and the new types of wines they developed have created new respect for Tuscan vintages: full-bodied *cuvées*, some made up of the newly planted French grapes, others pure Chiantis that are nevertheless aged in roughly 225-liter (60-gallon) *barriques*, as in the Bordelais. These *barrique* wines designated vini da tavola (table wines)—Marchese Mario Incisa's sassicaia, Marchese Piero Antinori's tignanello and solaia, Marchese Lodovico Antinori's ornellaia, the fontalloro of Felsina, and the tavernelle of Banfi—have restored Tuscany to its former preeminence in the world of wine.

Umbria

The wine region that encompasses the upper reaches of the Tiber is hilly country similar to the landscape of Tuscany, but its wines do not enjoy an international reputation. This is mainly because it has been rather timid in its recent efforts to improve quality. In the sixteenth century the wines of Castello, Todi, and Orvieto were considered exceptional, and steps are now being taken to return them to their former stature. The prime mover in Umbria is Giorgio Lungarotti, who by his own example and as an active advisor has managed to improve the Orvieto, raising the small area around Torgiano to first rank. He is now trying to achieve a similar success for other Umbrian wine regions.

The Marches

The Marches are like a vast garden sloping toward the sea. The fertile coastal strip between the Apennines and the Adriatic, from

Pesaro to Ascoli, with Ancona in the center, was the historical buffer between the medieval Holy Roman Empire to the north and the Papal States to the south. As is the case with many regions with mild climates, its wines tend to be voluptuous and mellow, without any tartness. Connoisseurs lament their resulting flatness. One exception is the verdicchio, a fresh, racy white wine with a pleasant fruitiness, the best examples of which come from Castelli di Jesi, Matelica, and Serrapetrona. This is a wine that wholly deserves its international triumph in the past few years.

Campania

As a wine-growing region, Rome's Campania Felix, the "blessed land" around the Gulf of Naples, now extends roughly fifty miles (80 kilometers) inland. Its enological heritage of ancient settlement by Greeks and Latins has survived the political upheavals of this contested landscape. The wines of the region still carry echoes of the early inhabitants in their names: Greco di Tufo, Fiano di Avellina, and Taurasi in the interior, Lacryma Christi on the coast. The first evidences of a new striving for quality by some of the area's winegrowers are deep, dark reds full of character and lively, fruity whites. The horrors of mass production are not fully overcome, but new standards have been set.

Basilicata

At first glance, the mountainous landscape of the Basilicata has nothing romantic about it: bare rock-strewn hills lie beige and brown under the scorching sun, punctuated only by occasional small hamlets and green fields. The Mezzogiorno—poor, dry, thinly populated—is a landscape for loners or for immigrants used to nothing better where they came from. The Greeks who settled the Basilicata from Tarentum more than twenty-five hundred years ago were not dismayed by the harshness of their new home. They dug wells, planted small vineyards, and left to their descendants the aglianico vine, known historically as *Vitis hellenica*. It is now the basis for one of the best red wines of southern Italy, with a fruity aroma, a firm, harmonious body, and an aftertaste that is at first abrupt but then becomes supple and intense. Aglianico is cultivated mainly in the vicinity of the village of Rionero, at the foot of Monte Vulture, which was already an important wine-trading center in the Middle Ages.

SARDINIA

The inhabitants of this Mediterranean island are known to have been winegrowers back in the Stone Age. Ruled successively by Phoenicians, Carthaginians, Romans, and later Byzantines, Moors, Genoese, Pisans, and Venetians, Sardinia finally fell to the Spanish, who introduced methods that made its wines much like those of Jerez or Madeira. Each new conqueror introduced new vines, so that now the island has an astonishing variety of them. For roughly forty years the Sardinians have emphasized concerted action and quality. They have developed a cooperative system in which they produce mainly a light, tingling white wine from the nuraghus grape, which is now thought of as *the* wine of Sardinia. Nevertheless, there are a few holdouts who allow their wines to develop a full flavor and wealth of character.

SICILY

The largest island in the Mediterranean is also Italy's largest winegrowing region, if not its most important one. The majority of Sicily's production is consumed locally or exported to northern Europe for blending. But, as in every other region in Italy, there are a few quality fanatics who demonstrate what superb wines can be produced with a sunny, Mediterranean climate, ample moisture, fertile soil, and a winegrowing tradition that reaches back into the mists of prehistory. Linguists tell us that the word *vino* itself comes from Sicily. The island produces not only noble dessert wines like marsala and other malvasia and muscat products but also nicely balanced dry wines from chardonnay, sauvignon, cabernet, and any number of indigenous vine varieties—successful compromises between rich extracts and acid.

Winegrowing Regions

AUSTRIA

SWITZERLAND

ALTO ADIGE–TRENTINO

VAL D'AOSTA

FRIULI–VENEZIA GIULIA

Po

LOMBARDY

VENETO

PIEDMONT

EMILIA ROMAGNA

LIGURIA

Arno

THE MARCHES

TUSCANY

UMBRIA

ABRUZZI

Tiber

MOLISE

LATIUM

APULIA

CAMPANIA

SARDINIA

BASILICATA

CALABRIA

SICILY

Using This Guide

———◆———

$\mathscr{J}$n the following listings we have divided the producers of grappa—and of acquavite d'uva—into vintners and distilleries, even though the distinctions between the two are often somewhat blurred. There are plenty of wine makers who have developed major distilling operations in which they purchase pomaces from their neighbors and who could legitimately be placed among the distilleries. On the other hand, there are distilleries that own their own vineyards. Trademarks that have become so well known that the producer's name is forgotten have further confused the picture.

To look up "your" grappa, turn first to the index that begins on page 261. There you'll find an alphabetical listing of vintners, distilleries, and brand names that are not given a heading of their own—for example, the grappa Fior di Vite, which is discussed under the distillery Ramazzotti. It is our hope that by separating vintners from distilleries we can provide you with a better overview of the grappa landscape.

Distilleries, especially large ones, generally have different goals in mind for their grappas; they care about qualities that will appeal to large numbers of buyers and have the ability to create first-class grappas even using mass-production methods. By treating them separately we certainly do not mean to belittle these "grappa factories."

Vintners tend to be especially committed to the winegrowing traditions of their region and to their own establishments, often centuries old. In their grappas they try to express the virtues of their local area, their individual understanding of wine, their own style. For them grappa is a by-product, though one that is becoming increasingly important. Vintners have worked hard to catch up with the old, established distilleries, and some of them have become innovators within the grappa culture. We hoped to acknowledge this by listing them separately.

A brief word about the tasting notes. We deliberately rejected the introduction of points, stars, or other rating devices. We have presented only high-quality grappas, most of them the very top brands. Distinguishing between them should be left to individual taste. This group of divas can be mercurial, and they are forever revealing new aspects of their personalities. Their rich flavors are composed of several hundred aromatics; each taster will appreciate only a limited number. It seemed presumptuous to try to squeeze these temperamental stars into some kind of rating corset.

There is no denying certain personal preferences, which can be read between the lines, but our tasting notes are mainly intended to capture at least the basic character of a given grappa. Others might well emphasize different features or discover new aspects of the aroma that we either failed to notice or considered less important.

We will be delighted if our subjective impressions inspire you to go back to familiar brands and taste them again more critically and if even connoisseurs find new delights in our selection. Our aim is to provide all grappa lovers with the background they need to make new discoveries of their own.

Vintners
A *to* Z

AIOLA

Fattoria della Aiola
Località Vagliagli
53010 Siena, Tuscany

*A*bulwark for the city of Siena in its wars against Florence in the thirteenth century, the Fattoria Aiola was turned into a classic Tuscan country manor, complete with farm buildings and owner's villa, in the seventeenth century. It lies in the heart of the Chianti Classico region. Giovanni Malgodo modernized his estate between 1968 and 1985, enlarging and remodeling its cellars, in which he ages not only Chianti Classico DOCG but also the

The vineyard landscape of Tuscany, home of many great grappas

white Val d'Arbia DOC, a botrytis-sweetened vin santo, and the modern vino da tavola Logaiolo, pressed from cabernet grapes.

GRAPPA VECCHIA RISERVA

Distilled at Bonollo's in Formigine in the traditional manner in steam alembics from sangiovese pomaces fermented with the must; aged for more than a year in wooden barrels and marketed at 100 proof in a limited edition of 2,430 handsomely designed bottles.
Our sample no. 2,180: A light blond distillate with a bouquet characterized by warm secondary aromas of vanilla, caramel, and roasted notes; like a cappuccino on the palate, warm coffee with milk and a hint of creamy, powdered chocolate; substantial finish.

GRAPPA L'AIOLA

Distilled in the classic discontinuous process at Bonollo's from fresh pomaces of Chianti Classico, then bottled at 90 proof in 70 cl wine bottles.
A congenial brandy with a warm, winy taste; a well-rounded body rich in extracts; and delicate spicy notes in its soft finish.

ALTESINO

⊶◦⊷

**Azienda Agricola Altesino
Località Torrenieri
53028 Montalcino, Tuscany**

A picture-perfect Tuscan wine estate in the hills above Montalcino. A picturesque cypress drive leads to the ruins of the ancient Palazzo Altesi, with cool, vaulted cellars in its Roman foundations. Altesino has recently gained a reputation for pressing one of the best Brunello di Montalcinos. The estate enologists, Claudio Basla and Pietro Rivella, can rely on twenty-two hectares (54½ acres) of superior vineyards, most of them high on the slopes, offering the best conditions for the brunello variety sangiovese grosso. In addition to brunello, the brunello sibling Rosso di Montalcino, aged a shorter time, and the sangiovese-cabernet *cuvée* Alte d'Altesi are typical of the top-quality products from this region around Montalcino.

Grappa di Brunello (1992)

Discontinuously distilled three times at Gioacchino Nannoni's in pot stills of different sizes from fully fermented, still-moist pomaces of the brunello vine sangiovese grosso directly after pressing. After the prescribed aging, bottled at 84 proof (50 cl).

Very light gold tone; the bouquet contains strong notes of nuts and grasses over distinct but pleasant secondary aromas; intense flavor development from tart to bittersweet.

Harvest time in Tuscany

ANTINORI

Marchesi L. e P. Antinori
Piazza degli Antinori, 3
50123 Florence, Tuscany

*T*his is the house that revived winegrowing in Tuscany. The wines of the landscape between Florence and Siena owe their international stature in no small part to the courageous ideas of Marchese Piero Antinori, who owns the family business together with Marchese Lodovico. In the mid-1970s Antinori and his enologist Giacomo Tachis created a new and very modern version of Chianti Classico patterned after the great models of Bordeaux and Burgundy. He also bravely challenged the strictures imposed by law in order to develop new wine types with an international appeal.

Relying on his family name, a guarantee of quality since the fourteenth century, the marchese created the unusual Tignanello, which fell outside the range of legally recognized varieties and could therefore be marketed only as vino da tavola. It was a wine that unleashed a revolution and sparked a winemaking renaissance in Tuscany. The wine guru Hugh Johnson dubbed it a "prophetic" wine. It blended 20 percent cabernet with the classic Tuscan sangiovese grape, and the new *cuvée* was aged in the Bordelais manner in new oak barrels in the *barrique* size of 220 liters (58 gallons).

The second stellar wine of the house comes from the same vineyard south of San Casciano. It is Solaia, a *cuvée* of cabernet sauvignon and cabernet franc, the 1985 vintage of which was awarded 97 out of 100 points by the American wine expert Robert Parker, Jr. This was another positive experience with the French vine variety cabernet, which improved even Chianti. The 10 percent white vines prescribed for Chianti were likewise replaced by red cabernet sauvignon—with equally outstanding results.

Despite the size of the estate, with more than 330 hectares (815 acres) of vineyards and production of up to half a million bottles in good years, Antinori has managed to reach his goals, thanks to huge investments in vine research and aging techniques but above all by expanding cautiously and insisting on top quality.

Grappa di Tignanello (1992)

From pomaces of grapes from the Tignanello vineyard in the Chianti Classico region, near Mercatale Val di Pesa. Twenty percent cabernet sauvignon, 80 percent sangiovese. The pomace was fermented with the must and distilled with steam at the distillery in Casciano Val di Pesa (84 proof, 50 cl).

A restrained, bittersweet aroma with a breath of autumn—mushrooms, hay, herbs. Subdued strength in its nobly bitter taste, which builds to a long, vibrant finish. A noble brandy of elegant discretion.

ATTEMS

❀

Conti Attems
Località Lucinico
34070 Gorizia, Friuli

*A*n estate in the Collio, the hilly area north of the provincial town of Gorizia that produces the best Friuli wines, which has been in the possession of the counts Attems for a thousand years. The majority of the vineyards lie in superb sites on the Piedimonte del Calvario. Since 1935 the estate has been run by Conte Douglas Sigismondo Attems. A graduate agronomist and president of the local winegrowing consortium, he is an expert who has played a decisive role in establishing the present-day quality criteria for Friulian wines. His long years of experience also benefit the grappa of the house, which is distilled from select pomaces from grapes of the Lucinico Hills. Conte Attems oversees the distilling process himself.

Grappa di Casa Attems

Discontinuously distilled by Flavio Comar in his Distilleria Aquileia, which is very highly regarded by quality vintners. Bottled at 86 proof (1 liter).

A well-structured grappa with the rich aroma of a well-tended kitchen garden: caraway, herbs, sesame, sorrel, summer flowers. Complex taste development from freshness to bittersweetness.

AVIGNONESI

→o←

AVIGNONESI
VIA DI GRACCIANO NEL CORSO, 91
53045 MONTEPULCIANO, TUSCANY

*I*n Tuscany a virtual synonym for the racy, elegant vino nobile of the growing region around Montepulciano. The base of the operation, which now encompasses several different estates, stands in the center of the Old Town—a sixteenth-century palazzo, in the cellars of which are aged, in addition to the famous red wine of the area, Chianti and wines from chardonnay, cabernet sauvignon, sauvignon blanc, and merlot.

The botrytis-sweetened vin santo from Avignonesi is absolutely first class, especially the very rare Occhio di Pernice, a sumptuous dessert wine with a fully harmonized sweetness and a strong corset of acid. In addition, the house has established itself as a pacesetter in the development of modern vini da tavola with its Il Marzocco, Vignola, and Grifi.

GRAPPA DA UVA DI VINO NOBILE

Distilled at Nannoni's from the fresh, very moist pomaces of the prugnolo gentile, a sangiovese variety. Distilled three times over steam in different alembics; after aging for six months, bottled at the distillery at 84 proof (50 cl).

Flower-scented, abundant nose with hints of resin, harmonious in taste and well structured. A grappa with a clear line of development from its first nuanced aroma to its intense finish.

BADIA A COLTIBUONO

BADIA A COLTIBUONO
LOCALITÀ BADIA A COLTIBUONO
53013 GAIOLE IN CHIANTI, TUSCANY

*T*he Badia a Coltibuono, or Abbey of the Good Harvest, was founded more than a thousand years ago, when monks from the monastery laid the foundations for successful winegrowing in the Chianti region between the Arno and Arbia Valleys. For the past century and a half the abbey and its vineyards have been owned by the family of Piero Stucchi Prinetti, whose marriage to the well-known cookbook author Lorenza de' Medici revived the old connection to the one-time owners from the Florentine ducal family. The estate's superb wines and its lovely grappa can be sampled in a charming tasting room.

GRAPPA DI BADIA A COLTIBUONO (1996)

From pomaces of the riserva *quality Chianti Classico. Distilled twice in single batches at Bruno Franceschini's in Cavaion in a limited edition of 3,387 bottles and aged beyond the minimum time required by law (80 proof, 70 cl).*

❙ *Brusque, masculine distillate with refreshing characteristics: bittersweet notes of citrus and nuts dominate the extremely harmonious aroma structure. Striking strength on the palate—a well-balanced bundle of energy.*

Cabernet, a classic red wine grape

BANEAR

<small>◆◇◆</small>

Aziende Agricole Friulane Banear
Località Treppo Grande
33010 Udine, Friuli

A conglomerate of several large estates in Friuli–Venezia Giulia. Their vineyards lie in the heart of the wine region—the Collio, the Colli Orientali, and the Grave del Friuli, the largest DOC area in Friuli. The region extends across the entire hinterland from the boundary with the Veneto to the edge of the Alps near Trieste. The Collio encompasses the vineyard sites around the former archbishopric of Görz (modern Gorizia) along the Slovenian border—they are the oldest and considered the best in Friuli–Venezia Giulia. Similarly good conditions are found in the Colli Orientali, or "Eastern Hills," to the north.

The Collio and the Colli Orientali are white wine country. The medium-sized Banear winery, with a cellar capacity of a million hectoliters (roughly 3½ million cubic feet), makes spritzig (slightly fizzy), youthful white wines from chardonnay, white burgundy, sauvignon blanc, and tocai friulano. Its enologists (under director Castellarin Argo Atal) also create the white wine classics of the region: a single-variety verduzzo in the manner of a recioto from partially dried grapes and picolit. A white grape native to the Colli Orientali, picolit is one of the once legendary but now almost vanished nineteenth-century varieties; it yields a hearty, highly expressive dessert wine with a pleasant, slightly bitter finish. In addition, they also make red wines from cabernet sauvignon and cabernet franc that are aged in *barriques*.

The estate's grappas are marketed under the name Villa Aba. Distillation, exclusively from their own pomaces, is accomplished within twenty-four hours of the end of fermentation in classic small copper alembics so as to achieve the purest result possible.

Villa Aba Grappa di Sauvignon (1994)

Single-variety distillate from sauvignon blanc pomaces, distilled twice and harmonized in stainless steel (84 proof, 50 cl).

♟ *A light, herbal bouquet and surprisingly flowery, winy body characterize this unusual, highly charming brandy.*

Villa Aba Grappa di Refosco (1994)

Single-variety distillate from refosco pomaces, twice distilled and harmonized in glass flasks (84 proof, 50 cl).

♟ *Richly aromatic brandy with a refined early summer bouquet and strong body with delicate acid accents.*

Additional Grappas
Grappa di Chardonnay
Grappa di Cabernet

BANFI

————◦————

Villa Banfi s.r.l.
Località Sant'Angelo Scalo
53024 Montalcino, Tuscany

This large estate of more than 710 hectares (1,754 acres) of vineyards was conjured up out of the Tuscan earth in the mid-1970s by the American wine importers Harry and John Mariani. They were assisted by the top enologist Ezio Rivella, who in short order brought Villa Banfi to the very first rank. Each year the estate produces 125 different wines, many of them—like the highly aromatic but low acid, almost perfumelike Chardonnay Fontanelle or the sweet, bubbly moscadello—oriented toward American tastes.

Unquestionably one of its top wines is its Brunello di Montalcino, aged in large oak barrels. Often compared to Château Pétrus and Romanée Conti wines, it has set new standards in Tuscany: a robust bouquet with distinct but delicate fruit and spicy notes, a round, velvety body with substantial structure, and a concentrated abundance of flavor.

Grappa di Brunello di Montalcino

Distilled in single batches in traditional pot stills from pomaces of the brunello vine sangiovese that have completely fermented in the mash. Aged on the estate for more than a year in small barrels of various woods, including oak and the classic grappa wood chestnut (90 proof, 50 cl).

Light blond with golden highlights and with vanilla and grapes in its bouquet; a round, pliant body with increasingly intense bitterness and a full and fruity finish.

GRAPPA DI MOSCADELLO

Distilled in single-batch small stills at Bonollo's from the further fermented pomaces of the muscat grapes of the traditional Moscadello di Montalcino and aged for more than a year in small barrels of oak and chestnut (90 proof, 50 cl).

▲ *A medium-heavy grappa with a fresh, grassy aroma and spicy notes; developing fruity, ripe orange tones on the palate.*

GRAPPA DI CHARDONNAY

Distilled in single-batch small stills at Bonollo's from the further fermented pomaces of late harvest chardonnay grapes (90 proof, 50 cl).

▲ *Elegant, aromatic, complex distillate with a grassy, summery aroma; a winy fullness on the palate with strong, slightly bitter spicy notes. Becomes more intense toward the finish.*

Additional Grappas

GRAPPA DI BRACHETTO

▲ *Single-variety grappa from pomaces from Banfi's Piedmont vineyards; strong bouquet, long finish.*

GRAPPA DI CABERNET

▲ *Single-variety grappa with a fragile nose, a body that becomes increasingly warmer, and an intense finish.*

GRAPPA DI GAVI

▲ *Single-variety grappa from pomaces from Banfi's Piedmont holdings; herb-toned aroma, quite neutral, straightforward body, and a delicate, medium-long finish.*

BARBERANI

AZIENDA AGRICOLA VALLESANTA DI LUIGI BARBERANI
LOCALITÀ CERRETO
05023 BASCHI, UMBRIA

*U*mbria's chains of hills are similar in climate and soil to those of neighboring Tuscany—and like their colleagues to the west, though not to such an extent, Umbria's innovative growers have managed to adapt to the international style.

One of them is Luigi Barberani. His estate was probably already in existence in Roman times. In the Middle Ages it was known as the Castello di Monticelli, but now it is called Vallesanta. One of its main products is the Orvieto DOC, but it also has vineyards planted with sémillon, cabernet, pinot noir, and sauvignon, from which Barberani creates interesting *cuvées* like foresco or the white pomaio. An old Orvieto tradition is preserved in the Muffe Nobile Calcaia, a golden blond, botrytis-sweet wine with a rich bouquet whose pomaces are used for the house grappa.

GRAPPA CALCAIA

Grappa from pomaces especially rich in sugar and extracts, thanks to botrytis. Distilled three times at low temperatures at Nannoni's in Paganico and aged for more than a year in oak barrels (84 proof, 50 cl).

A shimmer of old gold; masculine, spicy bouquet with a touch of honey that continues, becoming sweeter, up into the intense finish: a dessert brandy full of elegance and finesse.

BARBI

A classic Tuscan *fattoria* with a pigsty and butcher shop, a cheese shop and herds of sheep, a bakery, an oil press, an apiary, and a tavern in addition to the winery. The tavern serves solid, traditional dishes based on the estate's own products. Francesca Colombini's ancestors were already paying taxes on their *fattoria* near Montalcino back in the sixteenth century, and they were famed for their hospitality even then.

Still, the main emphasis of the large estate is on winegrowing—specifically brunello, the classic wine of Montalcino. The Barbi brunello won its first medal a hundred years ago, and countless awards have followed. Francesca Colombini has been in charge of the fattoria since 1974. Known as the "Lady of Brunello," the enologist has been repeatedly honored for her commitment to winegrowing and is much sought after at important conferences and congresses as an expert on Italian wine.

Her *fattoria* has profited from her international exchange: single-vineyard brunellos, carefully crafted *cuvées, barrique*

aging, and designer wines are now part of the Barbi program. All of this is in contrast to the grappa of the house: "We have deliberately kept the rustic character," Francesca Colombini explains. For her, country pleasures are part of a way of life that has a "human dimension," one that she feels has been lost in the cities. "We value the bonds of friendship, take part in the continuous struggle between man and nature. We love sitting by a fire in the fireplace, conversing, and now and again taking a sip of Grappa dei Barbi, an ideal and charming, always cheering comrade." Francesca Colombini has preserved an idyll we thought had been lost.

GRAPPA DEI BARBI DI BRUNELLO

Distilled in small batches at Bonollo's, then aged in used oak barrels just briefly, so that it does not take on color (90 proof, 70 cl).

A grappa full of chic and grandezza, with a complex aroma of nuts, fruit, grapes, and toast scents in its bouquet and taste and with a pure, slightly sweet finish. It brings to mind Tuscany's Indian summer with its cool morning fog.

BIANCHI

◄─◦►─

Azienda Agricola Giuseppe Bianchi
Via Roma, 37
28070 Sizzano, Piedmont

*T*his small family estate on the eastern edge of the Piedmont in the hilly landscape around Novara produces scarcely more than 40,000 bottles a year. Its specialty is a botrytis-sweet dessert wine from erbaluce, a variety indigenous to this region. The grapes are air dried in large baskets following the Passito method, in order to increase the percentage of fruit sugar and extracts. The single-variety grappa of the house is made from the pomaces of this wine fermented with the must.

Grappa di Vitigno Erbaluce

Distilled in single batches at Revel Chion's in Chiaverano in limited quantity, then bottled in 50 cl bottles at 80 proof.

🍷 *Our sample no. 2717: An astonishingly lively grappa with a lush, highly concentrated fruit bouquet of pears and plums, a soft, medium-heavy body, and a pleasantly bitter finish.*

BOLLA

FRATELLI BOLLA
PIAZZA CITTADELLA, 3
37122 VERONA, VENETO

A huge operation with extensive vineyards of its own stretching across the Veneto for more than sixty kilometers (thirty-seven miles). Ever since the house was established at the end of the last century, it has constantly sought to develop better international marketing strategies. Bolla has become synonymous with quality on all five continents, primarily for its excellent soaves produced in large quantities. In the United States the producer has become virtually synonymous with spritzig white wine from Soave and its neighboring villages in the province of Verona. Vineyard control over its three hundred contract wine-growers, careful grape selection, the most up-to-date techniques, and its considerable capital enable the concern to produce, in addition to the standard qualities, the single-vineyard soaves Castellaro and Frosca, Valpolicella Classico, and a number of top-quality red *cuvées* allowed to ferment a long time in the mash and aged in *barriques* of French Nevers oak. The two new table wines of the Creso line have found praise in blind tastings.

Bolla is somewhat more conservative in its distillation of grappa. The house prefers using pomaces of grape varieties that are grown in no other region of Italy. The single-vineyard Soave Castellaro grappa is made, for example, from pomaces of the white garganega grape to which a small quantity of trebbiano has been added. The red corvina is also grown solely for the regional valpolicella. At Bolla they press from it the valpolicella specialty amarone, whose fully fermented pomaces are also used for distilling grappa. They also produce an acquavite d'uva from fermented whole amarone grapes.

GRAPPA DI AMARONE

From pomaces of the Amarone di Valpolicella fermented with the must and discontinuously distilled at Bruno Franceschini's in Cavaion (86 proof, 50 cl).

An altogether lovely grappa with warm aromas of compote, chestnuts, toasted almonds, nuts, and caramel, nutty on the palate with a hint of bitter chocolate; very dry but long finish.

ACQUAVITE D'UVA

Discontinuously distilled in double-bottomed copper stills at Roner's in Bolzano from whole grapes of the Amarone di Valpolicella (86 proof, 50 cl).

Tentative nose, grapy, reminiscent of brandy, subtly fresh with a breath of mint; becoming sweeter, with spicy notes at the finish.

Additional Grappa
GRAPPA DI CASTELLARO

Reserve water tanks in a Piedmont vineyard

BRICCO MONDALINO

◀◦▶

Azienda Agricola Bricco Mondalino
Località Mondalino
15049 Vignale Monferrato, Piedmont

Two red vines, barbera and grignolino, dominate the Monferrato range, the heart of the Piedmont. The winegrower Gaudio Amilcare was especially fond of these traditional varieties and it is thanks to his efforts above all that grignolino has regained its former stature. His son Mauro, now the owner of the twelve-hectare (thirty-acre) vineyard, has continued his father's constant search for better quality. In addition to his classic grignolino he now produces the single-vineyard grignolino Bricco Mondalino, a well-structured wine that proves the possibilities of this often underrated grape. He makes two different qualities from his barbera grapes as well. His botrytis-sweet Casorzo, from malvasia grapes, is a lovely classic.

Grappa di Malvasia

Distilled on the estate in its steam-heated still from the botrytis-sweetened, thoroughly fermented pomaces of the Malvasia di Casorzo d'Alba (84 proof, 50 cl).

A clean, slightly earthy grappa, with an aroma-intensive, fruity nose that seems almost perfumed, with slightly acid herbal tones; an aldehyde-dry body and a sweetish, somewhat subdued but enormously aromatic finish with an echo of fresh herbs.

CAPARZO

⎯◦►⎯

AZIENDA AGRICOLA TENUTA CAPARZO
LOCALITÀ TORRENIERI
53028 MONTALCINO, TUSCANY

*A*n estate put together by the judicious purchase of various vineyards over the course of the recent renaissance of wine making in Tuscany. Now, after major investments, it is one of the better-known wine producers. The land around the manor house, the actual Tenuta Caparzo, was already settled in antiquity; on historical maps one finds it identified as "Ca' Pazzo," or House of the Fool. Caparzo now encompasses thirty-five hectares (eighty-six acres) of vineyards in the village of Montalcino, of which twenty-six (sixty-four acres) are planted with brunello. Most of the vineyards lie right around the manor house at an elevation of 220 meters (722 feet) and profit from the local climate, with dry summers and adequate rain in spring and fall. Thanks to determined further development in the vineyards and the cellar under the direction of the experienced advisor Vittorio Fiore, the estate is now producing, in addition to the standard qualities, a single-vineyard brunello that is one of the best from the region.

The Brunello di Montalcino La Casa is aged in *barriques* after long fermentation in the mash and thus develops the strong fruit bouquet, the well-structured body, and the long durability that distinguish great red wines.

The *cuvée* Le Grance—composed of chardonnay, sauvignon, and traminer—ages in *barriques* of Allier oak. It is one of the heavy, extra-rich white wines so valued by Vittorio Fiore that, when fully aged, can approach the ideal of a Montrachet. The pomaces of the brunello and the *cuvée* Le Grance are fermented with the must; after racking, they are transported under refrigeration to the famous Brunello distillery, where they are immediately processed.

Grappa di Brunello

Distilled twice with steam in copper steam stills (86 proof, 70 cl).

A well-filled nut basket: hazelnuts, walnuts, even slightly bitter creamy Brazil nuts in the rich bouquet, in addition to autumnal notes that persist, soft and round, well into the long finish. A highly unusual, elegant brandy of great complexity.

Grappa di Chardonnay Le Grance (1992)

After being distilled twice in copper alembics, the distillate was aged for two years in barriques of Allier wood previously used for aging wine (86 proof, 50 cl).

Radiant amber color; summer fresh aroma of citrus fruits, nuts, and a touch of sorrel; faintly sweet wood tannins underscore the elegant freshness of the gentle finish.

An old castle in Tuscany

CAPEZZANA

—◦►—

Tenuta di Capezzana
Località Seano, Via di Capezzana 100
50040 Carmignano, Tuscany

*A*n estate with a long history—they have been growing wines here for nearly twelve hundred years. Today the estate is owned by the aristocratic Contini Bonacossi family. The head of the house, Conte Ugo, in collaboration with the enologist Alberto Bramini, champions the tradition-rich but modern wines from Carmignano, which have been protected by their own DOCG since 1990. The demonstrably long history of growing cabernet sauvignon here—the vine was introduced centuries ago by an ancestor from Bordeaux—allows the Carmignano growers to round out their Chianti with cabernet perfectly legally—setting an example for the entire production of Chianti Classico.

Grappa di Capezzana (1992)

Distilled at Gioacchino Nannoni's in Paganico from pomaces of the red carmignano ghiaie della furba, aged fifteen months in barriques of Limousin oak (84 proof, 50 cl).
A warm, soft distillate with a complex, round, fruity aroma and tremendous presence on the palate. Nutty and tart with a subtle play of tastes, dry finish. Highly unusual and quite successful.

Additional Grappa
Grappa di Vin Santo (1997)

CAPRAI

Val di Maggio A. Caprai
Località Torre
06036 Montefalco, Umbria

*T*here is history everywhere you turn here. Around the small estate belonging to Arnaldo Caprai lie vineyards praised by Pliny the Elder, known to have been protected by strict laws already in the fifteenth century and now planted with sagrantino, the traditional grape variety of the region. From it Arnaldo and his son Marco produce the Sagrantino di Montefalco, a regional wine specialty that was only recently accorded the designation DOCG. For all their pride in enological tradition, they are also open to modern pressing and aging methods: the Grechetto dei Colli Martani, called "Grecante," is aged in *barriques*, which brings out the best of the Greek grechetto grape with its substantial, nutty character. The two grappas of the house reflect its signature: first-class pomaces, a good distillery master, careful aging, and elegant packaging. These are first-rate grappas.

Grappa Gran Riserva di Sagrantino

From only lightly pressed and therefore very moist pomaces of the red sagrantino grape, distilled in single batches at Bonollo's in Modena and aged in small oak barrels (90 proof, 50 cl).

🍷 *A light blond distillate with an aroma development from fresh to ripe fruit, consistent development on the palate from sweet to bitter, and a long finish.*

Additional Grappa
Grappa di Grechetto

Assisi, in the heart of Umbria's winegrowing region

CARPENÈ MALVOLTI

Carpenè Malvolti
Via A. Carpenè, 1
31015 Conegliano, Veneto

*O*ne of the leading spumante producers in Italy, with
tremendous importance as a vineyard as well. In addition
to a dry spumante, which wine critic Horst Dohm has called
one of the "most distinguished examples of the *metodo classico*
spumantes," it produces mainly the up-to-date Prosecco di
Conegliano. It was actually the founder of the firm, the chemist
Antonio Carpenè, who discovered the value of the prosecco
grape for sparkling wine and developed a tank fermentation
process now considered standard—the Charmat method, which
preserves the fruity freshness of prosecco better than the classic
bottle fermentation method. The firm's name has therefore become synonymous with prosecco in Italy.

In addition, the successful estate owner devoted himself to
wine-making theory, and in 1838 he founded Italy's first school for
viticulture and enology. Today the business is run by his grandson
Antonio, Jr., and great-grandson Etile, Jr. In addition to sparkling
wines, they produce perfectly respectable pinot wines: single-
variety chardonnays, pinot biancos, and red pinot neros.

The house grappas (all at 90 proof in 70 cl bottles) are freshly
distilled in its own distillery and presented in three versions: as a
young white Grappa Bianca, a three-year-old Fine Vecchia
Grappa, and a Grappa di Antica Annata, aged more than twenty-
five years in barrels of Slovenian oak and bottled in elegant porce-
lain flasks. The original bottle shape used for the two younger versions has a tradition: it was modeled after the bottle gourd
originally used as a grappa container, with a corncob as a stopper.

GRAPPA BIANCA

🍷 *An unusual grappa with a full, fruity bouquet; a fresh, youthful body; and an appealing light finish increasingly reminiscent of the pomace.*

GRAPPA CARPENÈ MALVOLTI

🍷 *Delicate gold color, appealing aroma with ripe fruits and a breath of vanilla; strong, but slightly sharp body that turns into a round sweetness in the finish. A fine digestive.*

Additional Grappa
FINE VECCHIA GRAPPA
Straw yellow white-wine grappa aged at least three years in small oak barrels.

CASTAGNOLI

FATTORIA CASTAGNOLI
LOCALITÀ CASTELLINA IN CHIANTI
53011 SIENA, TUSCANY

*S*uccessful advertising professional tosses it all in and becomes a winegrower in Tuscany—a familiar enough tale in the last few years. For the Swabian Hans Joachim Döbbelin it was only a hobby at first, but now it is his great passion. On his small estate everything is done organically, using the most modern technology and, at harvest time, the help of his friends. The result is a Chianti from first-class, healthy grapes that can hold its own against the products of his highly decorated neighbors.

The grappa of the house was originally intended only for the folks who provided extra help when needed. Today it is an essential chapter in Döbbelin's Tuscan success story.

GRAPPA PER AMICI

Distilled immediately after racking from the very moist sangiovese pomaces of Chianti Classico fermented with the must at the neighboring distiller Gioacchino Nannoni's in Paganico (84 proof, 75 cl).

Summer rain grappa: aroma of wet grass, mushrooms, fruit, becoming intense on the palate; a dried-fruit accent in the finish.

CASTELGIOCONDO

Tenuta di Castelgiocondo
Località Castelgiocondo
53024 Montalcino, Tuscany

The estate in Montalcino is owned by the Marchesi di Frescobaldi. More than 200 hectares (494 acres) of its total of 850 hectares (2,100 acres) are planted in grapes. Mostly they grow the classic brunello grape, sangiovese grosso, but for some years they have also been successful with cabernet sauvignon and merlot, from which they create the well-structured vino da tavola *cuvées* for which Tuscany is internationally famous. In collaboration with the California wine pioneer Mondavi, they have also produced for several years the Luce *cuvée* of sangiovese and merlot, which has brought them additional renown. The grappa of the house is made from the pomaces of the Brunello di Montalcino.

Grappa di Brunello di Montalcino

Distilled in single batches at Bonollo in Greve in Chianti from pomaces of Brunello di Montalcino fermented with the wine (90 proof, 70 cl).

A light, amicable grappa with a spicy, floral, somewhat delicate and feminine character. Its rich structure is a virtual tapestry of aroma components with deep floral notes; highly concentrated, slightly peppery finish.

CASTLÈT

CASCINA CASTLÈT
STRADA CASTELLETTO, 6
14055 COSTIGLIOLE D'ASTI, PIEDMONT

*W*hen one thinks of the grape variety barbera, one immediately thinks of Barbera d'Asti. In the Piedmont, however, they say that while barbera may be popular with the Asti people, it runs in the very blood of the folks from Costigliole.

Cascina Castlèt is a family estate in the Asti hills, with ten hectares (twenty-five acres) of vineyards planted almost exclusively with barbera. It is managed by Mariuccia Borio, who brings her energy, a wealth of ideas, and a considerable professionalism to the various barbera variants, wines with their own personalities but deeply rooted in tradition. Labor-intensive care of the vines, modern pressing techniques, and long aging have assured the reputation of the Borio wines, which are never placed on the market until they are fully mature. In addition to

The family estate Cascina Castlèt in the Asti hills

her reds, she produces a delightful sparkling Moscato d'Asti DOCG—the muscat dessert wine typical of the area.

GRAPPA DI PASSUM

A grappa from gently pressed pomaces of the red wine specialty Passum: healthy barbera grapes are dried in open baskets for twenty days after harvest, concentrating their sugars and breaking down their acids. Distilled on the estate in its small double-bottomed pot still immediately after racking. Aged for a year in a stainless-steel tank and another six months in glass flasks (86 proof, 50 cl).

A clear, clean distillate; voluminous, intensely fruity aroma with a note of bittersweet and hints of compote and raisins; light, refreshing body, which gains strength in the long finish and ends with a bit of a bite.

Additional Grappas

GRAPPA DI AVIÉ

Also distilled from dried grapes immediately after racking. The glass-clear muscat grappa captivates with its intense fruit, normally achieved only in acquavite d'uva.

GRAPPA DI POLICARPO

Straw yellow barbera grappa aged in acacia wood barrels; intensely aromatic, with a dry, harmonious body.

CERETTO

---◦►---

Fratelli Ceretto
Località S. Cassiano, 34
12051 Alba, Piedmont

*B*runo and Marcello Ceretto would have to traverse the entire Langhe (heartland of the Piedmont) if they wished to visit all their vineyards and nurseries. The Ceretto brothers are traditionalists and innovators at the same time. By reducing fermentation and aging times they removed the tartness from the traditional barolos and barbarescos. They have planted internationally famous varieties and are the top producers of the botrytis-sweetened Moscato d'Asti. Distilled in their own facility, the Ceretto brothers' single-variety grappas present a lovely cross-section of wine making in the Piedmont.

Grappa Rossana (1994)

Distilled immediately after racking in a double-bottomed pot still from the red dolcetto pomaces of the Rossana slope in Alba (84 proof, 70 cl).

❧ *A fresh distillate with winy, spicy notes in its aroma; its taste develops into a pleasant bitterness with toasted aromas; soft, round body with a strong finish—a straightforward, respectable grappa.*

Additional Grappas
Grappa Zonchera Nebbiolo
Grappa Barolo Brunate

CHIARLO

MICHELE CHIARLO
STRADA STATALE NIZZA-CANELLI
14042 CALAMANDRANA, PIEDMONT

*M*ichele Chiarlo's story is typical. As a quality-conscious wine dealer, he began buying the best vineyards to realize his own ideal of top-quality modern wines. In addition to barolo and barbaresco, he is especially devoted to gavi, from which he produces intense and delightful wines by sharply reducing the yield and partially aging them in new oak barrels. As for his grappas, Chiarlo is a traditionalist. The reliable, aroma-rich muscat grapes of the Moscato d'Asti provide the pomaces.

GRAPPA DI MOSCATO D'ASTI

Distilled from muscat Asti Spumante pomaces in single batches in small copper stills at the small Luigi Bossi distillery in Cuneo (84 proof, limited to 1,100 75 cl bottles).

Our sample bottle no. 404: An aromatic powerhouse with an overwhelming muscat scent; a liqueurlike sweetness in taste, which harmonizes with desserts of all kinds.

Additional Grappas
GRAPPA DI BARILOT
GRAPPA DI NEBBIOLO DA BAROLO
GRAPPA DI AIRONE
GRAPPA DI GAVI
LACRIME

CLERICO

Azienda Agricola Domenico Clerico
Località Manzoni-Cucchi 67
12065 Monforte d'Alba, Piedmont

*T*he Piedmontese vintner Domenico Clerico is one of the forward-looking growers of his region, even though—or perhaps because—he is a traditionalist. His knowledge of the centuries-old winegrowing tradition of the Piedmont has schooled his eye to the possibilities of specific sites and helped him produce a whole series of single-vineyard barolos of top quality. His masterpiece is the barolo from the vineyard Ciabot Mentin Ginestra, which is among the front-runners in blind tastings year after year. The pomaces of this barolo, fermented with the wine, are distilled into one of the best Piedmont grappas.

Grappa di Barolo

Distilled twice in single-batch, double-bottomed stills at the Rovero brothers' distillery in Asti from the nebbiolo pomaces of the single-vineyard Barolo Ciabot Mentin Ginestra and harmonized in stainless-steel tanks (98 proof, 50 cl).

A nutty, masculine distillate with a continuous line of development and dark, deeply vibrating strength supplemented by light floral notes. Outstanding and full of rustic elegance. A member of the landed gentry of grappas.

COLLAVINI

CASA VINICOLA E. COLLAVINI
MANIERO DI GRAMOGLIANO
VIA DELLA RIBOLLA GIALLA, 2
LOCALITÀ CORNO DI ROSAZZO
33040 UDINE, FRIULI

Collavini is one of the top producers, not only with respect to wines. A third of its output is made up of spumante, mostly produced according to the champagne method. For the present owner, Manlio Collavini (grandson of the founder of the estate, Eugenio), this was but one more step in a logical line of development. The Collavinis have spared no effort to make up-to-date wines of high quality. Very early on they planted the now more popular cabernet, pinot, and merlot along with native Friuli varieties. But in making his grappa Collavini adheres to old Friulian traditions: small-scale distilling in small alembics.

GRAPPA DI PINOT GRIGIO

Distilled in single batches from pinot grigio pomaces from the Colli Orientali del Friuli; aged for a year in stainless-steel tanks (86 proof, 70 cl).

An herb-toned, intense grappa with pleasant taste of ripeness with a developing touch of bitterness.

Additional Grappa
BORGO DEI ROSETI

D'ANGELO

Casa Vinicola D'Angelo
Via Provinciale, 8
85028 Rionero in Vulture, Basilicata

*T*his is one of the best wine makers of the Mezzogiorno region Basilicata, which is now no
longer important for its winegrowing. Donato and
Lucio D'Angelo are famous for their noble wines
from the ancient variety aglianico, but also grow malvasia, muscat, and Riesling.

 Their aglianico is produced in two versions: as a
traditionally produced, elegant Aglianico del Vulture
and as a noble *Auslese* called Canneto—the latter
with an intense color, a strong, almost liqueurlike
cherry tone in its fruity bouquet, and a harmonious, well-structured body. The pomaces of
both variants are distilled into grappa at Nannoni's in Paganico in Tuscany.

Grappa di Aglianico

*Distilled three times in small stills as soon as poss-
ible after fermentation with the mash (84 proof in
50 cl grappa bottles with an unfortunately problematic natural cork, which does not seal well).*

 *A pleasant, finely structured and dry grappa
with an aroma of flowers and spice; its delicate body surprises with its astonishing strength,
and its extract-rich finish delights with its harmonious spiciness. A distillate of great complexity for special occasions.*

DIEVOLE

Fattoria Dievole
Località Vagliagli
53010 Siena, Tuscany

*O*ne of the oldest wine estates in the Chianti Classico region, first cited in 1090. Sixteen different vineyards make up Dievole, each with its own vintner and each producing its own specific type of wine. All sixteen decide upon their common direction, growing methods, and eventual *cuvées* with Dievole's owner, Mario Schwenn.

Seventy percent of the harvest goes into Chianti Classico, of which 30 percent in turn is *riserva* quality. A fifth of the wines are offered as single-vineyard Chiantis from the vineyards in Sessina, Petrignano, and Campi Nuovi. The Dievole grappa is produced from the classic pomace mix of Chianti Classico.

Grappa di Chianti Classico (1994)

Distilled twice at Bonollo's in copper steam alembics from the traditional pomace cuvée of Chianti Classico, harmonized for six months in stainless steel (84 proof, 70 cl).

A profound, very complex distillate: aristocratic aroma, refreshing on the palate, with a delicate undertone of bitterness well into its long, spicy finish.

EBERLEHOF

*T*he Eberlehof, first documented in 1312, has been owned by the Zisser family since 1668. The small estate—now run according to ecological principles by the Zissers, father and son—owns vineyards in the best parts of the wine village St. Magdalena, near Bolzano in the Alto Adige.

Years of effort to restore the reputation of St. Magdalener, which had become known as a bulk wine, and the classic quality of their red, full-bodied wine have brought the Zissers numerous prizes in national and international wine competitions.

Grappa St. Magdalener

Grappa from the very moist pomaces of the red St. Magdalener mixture of schiava and Tschaggeler grapes, distilled in the traditional manner in single batches in a small still and bottled at 90 proof (70 cl).

A highly complex grappa with an earthy, floral character, with echoes of medicinal herbs; a late summer distillate with a delicately bitter finish.

Cortaccia in Alto Adige

ENDRIZZI

CASA VINICOLA ENDRIZZI
LOCALITÀ MASETTO
38010 SAN MICHELE ALL'ADIGE, TRENTINO

$\mathcal{O}$ ne of the old winegrowing families of the Trentino. In the Middle Ages their vineyards Masetto and Kinderleit belonged to the Augustinians, then later went to the counts of Thun. With a feeling for modern trends, the present owners, Paolo and Christine Endrici, have managed to attract the attention of both wine lovers and connoisseurs. They are among the producers who pay particular attention to the visual presentation of their wines, using elegant bottles in expensive packaging designed by Trentino artists. The same care, of course, goes into making their wines from the fashionable varieties chardonnay and cabernet sauvignon, which one of their ancestors had introduced at the end of the last century. Some of their vines are as much as fifty years old and, thanks to deliberate reduction of their yield, produce especially extract-rich grapes. Organic fertil-

Christine and Paolo Endrici

ization, harvest by hand in two stages, modern pressing techniques, and aging in *barriques*—nothing is too good for the wines of the "Collezione Endrizzi."

Grappa Chardonnay Trentino (1992)

Distilled in single batches in a double-bottomed pot still (84 proof, 50 cl). Label and packaging by the noted Trentino artist Giuseppe Debiasi.

A typical chardonnay grappa: reserved aroma with earthy mushroom notes, somewhat alcoholic on the palate, with a liqueurlike sweetness up into the long, ripe finish.

Additional Grappa

Grappa Cabernet Sauvignon

FASSATI

---◦---

FASSATI DI FAZI-BATTAGLIA S.P.A.
GRACCHIANO DI MONTEPULCIANO
53046 PIEVE DI SINALUNGA, TUSCANY

A wine-trading house founded in 1913, which early on earned a good reputation for the production and marketing of its high-quality wine Vino Nobile di Montepulciano. Its 1969 merger with the dynamic wine house Fazi-Battaglia opened up international contacts and with them set the stage for the worldwide marketing of Fassati wines. The classified Fassati vineyards occupy the best slopes of Montepulciano. As a result, the house concentrates on the production of vini nobili from specific vineyards, hoping to preserve their physiochemical and sensory individuality. Yield is limited to fifty hectoliters per hectare (seventy-two cubic feet per acre). The *cuvée* of the vino nobile is made up of the sangiovese variety prugnolo gentile for strength and richness of body and canaiolo nero for elegance and aroma; it is rounded out with roughly 20 percent of the white wine grapes

malvasia, trebbiano, and grecchetto. The two grappa variants of the house are produced from the pomaces of the vino nobile.

GRAPPA NOBILE

Distilled in single batches with steam at Bonollo's in Formigine (90 proof, handblown 70 cl blue glass flask).

Autumnal, floral distillate with a soft, aromatic character and fine structure.

GRAPPA NOBILE STRAVECCHIA

After distillation and the prescribed aging in stainless steel, this grappa ages an additional six to twelve months in barriques *of Slovenian oak (90 proof, handblown 50 cl bottle from a workshop in Florence).*

As light as white wine, with a deep aroma with well-integrated wood notes; winy on the palate, autumnal, with a pleasant nutty finish. A very elegant brandy.

FAZI-BATTAGLIA

FAZI-BATTAGLIA S.P.A.
CASTELPLANIO STAZIONE
60032 ANCONA, THE MARCHES

*O*ne of Italy's wine houses that recognized early on the value of careful marketing and elegant design. The now classic bottle inspired by antique amphorae was adopted in a 1953 design competition—a bottle that has since become the symbol of verdicchio wines from Castelli di Jesi, Matelica, and Serrapetrona. This harmony between product and packaging has made the verdicchio marketed under the brand name Titulus such an international success that the firm has been able to make massive investments in wine-making technology and new vineyards—in fact, it was forced to by its own success.

Today the house owns 280 hectares (692 acres) of vineyards, in which other wines in addition to verdicchio are grown with controlled origin designation. The purchase of the old, established wine house of Fassati in Chianti and two other top estates in Tuscany has expanded the Fazi-Battaglia portfolio to include Chianti Classico, Orvieto Classico, and above all Vini Nobili di Montepulciano.

The grappas of the house are produced from the verdicchio pomace from their own vineyards in Castelli di Jesi—it is gently pressed so as to preserve the moisture that accounts for the softness of the distillate.

Grappa di Verdicchio Stravecchia

Distilled in steam at the Distilleria Aquileia di F & A Comar and, after six months' aging in stainless-steel tanks, aged an additional year in barriques *of Slovenian oak. Bottled at 88 proof in a graceful variant of the verdicchio bottle (50 cl).*

Highly reliable, lovely grappa with a reasonably winy flavor and an autumnal bouquet of soil, hay, mushrooms; strong in taste, with slight animal notes and a long finish.

Additional Grappa

Grappa di Verdicchio di Castelli di Jesi

FELSINA

———◦►———

FATTORIA DI FELSINA
VIA NATIONALE CHIANTIGIANA, KM 484
53019 CASTELNUOVO BERARDENGA, TUSCANY

For the shipper and bank president Domenico Poggiali, the first sip in the small Castelnuovo trattoria was all it took. The wine had potential, and he would develop it. The next day—this was in 1964—he bought the vineyard it came from. His instinct had not betrayed him. Yet it would not become clear until years later what a treasure the novice enologist had acquired with his purchase of the Fattoria di Felsina and its vineyards.

From the start, Poggiali's decisions were crowned with success. His son-in-law Giuseppe Mazzocolin, up to that time a teacher of Greek and Latin in a big-city school but a passionate wine lover with a talent for organization, took over the direction of the 350-hectare (865-acre) estate with 50 hectares (124 acres) of vineyards together with the connoisseur and cellar master Franco Bernabei. A restructuring and enormous investments followed, and very soon great vintages as well. The rocky, chalky soil in the north of Tuscany, the unique microclimate, and Bernabei's *barrique* aging specific to each wine type produced wines of a highly individual character, wholly made to measure.

The early harvest, fresh Chardonnay I Sistri, for example, is only one of his remarkable wines. Others are the floral, well-rounded Isis from late harvested but healthy grapes; the botrytis-sweetened vin santo pressed from traditional air-dried grapes; a cabernet called Maestroraro; and especially the Fontalloro—a resounding sangiovese of such class that even the cellar masters of the Bordelais estates Pétrus, Margaux, and Cheval Blanc have made pilgrimages to Felsina to try to discover the Tuscan's secrets.

Simple accident? Or the result of deliberate experimentation? Doubtless more the latter. In any event, the first-class products of Felsina reflect great effort and relatively costly practices that have occasionally distressed Poggiali. But his fascination with developing top-quality wine by testing all possible nuances has also excited the calculating investor from Ravenna again and again, spurring him on.

Some day the Felsina team wants to establish an optimal vine lifetime and perfect production methods. But until then many ideas will be tested and many questions asked, and many vintages should provide them with answers. They have at least established their chief goal: producing the first unquestioned *premier cru* from Tuscany.

BERARDENGA GRAPPA CHIANTI CLASSICO (1992)

From Chianti Classico pomaces distilled with steam in a classic pot still at Comar's in Aquileia (80 proof, 75 cl).

A grappa with an intense, powerful aroma with almost excessive grapiness balanced by hints of fresh grapefruit. The long finish develops a spontaneous burst of pleasant, almost chocolate bitterness with fresh grassy notes. Lovely!

FEUDI

—◦►—

AZIENDA AGRICOLA FEUDI DI SAN GREGORIO
LOCALITÀ CERZA GROSSA
83050 SORBO SERPICO, CAMPANIA

*T*his estate founded by Luciano Ercolino and Mario Capaldo has been in existence only since 1986, yet its owners have been setting standards for the rest of the region for a long time. The Greeks and Romans made wines in this "Felix Campania" thousands of years ago, and Roman dignitaries found the area an ideal vacation spot, one that fulfilled their fantasies. Wine lovers now see theirs fulfilled here as well, for never have tradition and contemporary style come together so wonderfully as in the now almost legendary Serpico *cuvée.* Anyone traveling in Campania should definitely stop in; it is delightful to sit in the small tasting room and try the estate's delicious wines and other products.

GRAPPA DI GRECO DI TUFO

Distilled in the top Sicilian distillery of Giovanni Lo Fauci from pomaces of the single-variety Greco di Tufo (86 proof, 50 cl).
A light, fruity brandy with a floral, fruity nose and delightful, slightly bitter harmony on the palate. A refreshing distillate that is pleasing even as an aperitif.

GRAPPA DI AGLIANICO DI TAURASI

Distilled twice in single batches from aglianico, a variety introduced into southern Italy by the ancient Greeks (86 proof, 50 cl).
A deep, dark, vibrant brandy with distinct fruit aromas—bananas, peaches, raisins—and a powerful development on the palate. Spice notes—cloves, vanilla—accompany the chocolaty bitterness in the finish. An outstanding grappa.

GRAPPA DI FIANO DI AVELLINO

Distilled twice in single batches at the Giovi distillery in Sicily from the single-variety pomaces of Fiano di Avellino (86 proof, 50 cl).

A fresh, crisp distillate with piquant overtones (sorrel, citrus); appetizing, with strong floral notes. Unfortunately little stamina in the finish.

LE FILIGARE

FATTORIA LE FILIGARE
LOCALITÀ SAN DONATO IN POGGIO, VIA SICELLA 37
50021 BARBERINO VAL D'ELSA, TUSCANY

*T*his estate, which produces mainly heavy, velvety-soft red wines, occupies an old villa in the hills of the Elsa Valley north of Siena. The name derives from the Tuscan term for the ancient custom of decorating a manor house with torches *(fiaccole)* as a signal that the neighbors were invited to a drinking party. Today the enologists Carlo Burchi and Luciano Bandini can take pride in the fact that their wines are treasured not only in Tuscany but throughout the world. They mainly make Chianti Classico, but also the vino da tavola *cuvée* Podere Le Rocce from 65 percent sangiovese and 35 percent cabernet sauvignon, which is always delightful.

GRAPPA LE FILIGARE

Distilled from the estate's Chianti Classico pomaces at Nannoni's in Paganico (86 proof, 50 cl).

❦ *A highly complex and restrained grappa redolent of ripe fruits; dense and deeply resonant on the palate with a powerful body.*
It is necessary to give this distillate time; it develops its best qualities only after adequate contact with air.

Vineyards in the heart of Tuscany

FONTANAFREDDA

❖

Tenimenti di Barolo e Fontanafredda
Via Alba, 15
12050 Serralunga d'Alba, Piedmont

*F*irst a royal seat, then a count's estate, then a wine-
producing bank investment—one of the larger and more
important wine estates of the Piedmont.

For Victor Emmanuel II, Italy's king from the house of
Savoy, the villa with its heraldic colors of ocher and red and its
surrounding lands was more than simply an agricultural holding
and hunting preserve. His Majesty hunted a very special prey:
the lovely Rosa Vercellone, his mistress, became Countess Mirafiori e Fontanafredda and his morganatic spouse in 1869. Their
son and the heir to Fontanafredda, Count Emmanuele Guerrini
di Mirafiori, founded the wine estate in 1878; in 1929, at the time
of the world financial crisis, it passed to the bank Monte dei
Paschi di Siena. Bad for the aristocracy, good for aristocratic
wines: with the bank's capital, investments were made in vine-

The Piedmont, or foothills

yards, pressing techniques, and quality controls that smaller vintners can only dream of.

The results were stunning. Thanks to deliberate yield reduction and the use of traditional fermentation methods with long fermentation in the mash, the estate's eight high-carat barolos from the sites La Rosa, Gallaretto, Vigna Bianca, La Delizia, La Villa, Lazzarito, Gattinera, and San Pietro and its other wines from the classic alba varieties are now among the top Piedmont products. Also exquisite is the hand-picked Spumante La Rosa from the top Gattinera vineyard with its distinct *mousseux,* elegant aroma, strong body, and delicately sour finish.

Despite all the modern achievements and up-to-date marketing, Fontanafredda has preserved much of its old flair. Farm families live on the estate as they did a century ago, children are baptized here and holidays celebrated, not only at harvest time.

A fixed element of this tradition is grappa: produced with appropriate care from the fresh, moist pomaces of the nebbiolo varieties michet and lampia, the basis of the barolos of Fontanafredda.

Grappa di Nebbiolo da Barolo

Grappa distilled in the estate distillery from freshly racked barolo pomaces and aged for more than a year in oak barrels (90 proof, 70 cl).

Light golden color, deep aroma with toasted notes; winy in taste, with a pleasant bitter tone in the long, vibrant finish. A deep, round, but very gentle distillate.

FRATTINA

VILLA FRATTINA S.P.A.
LOCALITÀ GHIRANO DI PRATA
33080 PORDENONE, FRIULI

An estate founded by the counts Frattina four hundred years ago, now owned by the spirit producers Averna. In collaboration with the winegrowing institute in Conegliano, the people at Frattina have been experimenting for some years with newly developed or improved vine varieties, organic growing methods, and new pressing techniques.

New pressing methods have also benefited the estate's grappa production. The pomaces that reach the stills have been more gently pressed, and the results are gentler as well. Frattina does its own distilling, part of it in pot stills to achieve greater aroma, part of it continuously to produce lighter and purer brandies. After the aging prescribed by law, the distillery master blends the individual distillates separately according to grape variety, creating fine and very harmonious brandies.

GRAPPA DI TOCAI

A grappa cuvée *distilled from pomaces of the Friuli specialty tocai, carefully fermented after pressing (80 proof, 70 cl).*

A mellow, full-bodied grappa with a pleasantly spicy bouquet and ripe fruit notes.

GRAPPA DI CABERNET

Distilled from cabernet sauvignon pomaces fermented with the must (80 proof, 70 cl).

A light, elegant distillate with a ripe, slightly peppery summer bouquet of apples, pears, grapefruit; harmonious flavor development and pleasant, gentle finish.

Additional Grappas
GRAPPA DI CHARDONNAY
ACQUAVITE D'UVA RIESLING *(handblown bottle, 50 cl)*

GABBIANO

CASTELLO DI GABBIANO
VIA DI GABBIANO, 22
50024 MERCATALE DI VAL DI PESA, TUSCANY

A typical Tuscan estate: during the late Middle Ages it was expanded into a *castello* by noble families as protection against marauding soldiers. It produced Chiantis without distinction for centuries, but that changed when the Milanese wine-making novice Rino Arcaini bought the *castello*.

His main interest is in classic Chianti, but soon he was producing more unusual wines as well. A single-variety sangiovese, for example, that bears the name of his oldest daughter, Ania; a chardonnay called Ariella after his second daughter; and finally the cabernet sauvignon R&R, using his own initials and those of his wife, Raynelle. The estate's pomaces are distilled at the Nannoni distillery in Paganico.

GRAPPA DI ANIA

Distilled three times and given time to mature in oak barrels after six months' aging in stainless steel (84 proof, 50 cl).

A fine grappa for the Christmas season: gold colored, with the strong, spicy aroma of Lebkuchen (cinnamon, nutmeg, cloves), a harmonious, mature, rounded body, and a gentle finish.

Additional Grappa
GRAPPA DI ARIELLA

Tuscany's hill country

GAJA

---◦---

ANGELO GAJA
VIA TORINO, 36/A
12050 BARBARESCO, PIEDMONT

*A*ngelo Gaja is the Piedmont's visionary wine maker. It is said that at the age of eighteen he paid no attention to wine and at twenty-five was making his living in a snack bar, yet only twenty years later he changed the course of wine making in his homeland. It makes a good story, but in fact Gaja comes from a family of winegrowers and wine dealers in Barbaresco. As the son of the mayor, Giovanni Gaja, he grew up on a well-organized estate with its own cellar and vineyard master. His father, a clever businessman with a keen sense of timing, managed to buy top-quality vineyards until he had some sixty hectares (148 acres) and more than forty employees. In 1959 the man who would inherit the estate attended the wine-making school in Alba, even though he would later stand aloof from enological developments.

Angelo first got a taste of the wider world by frying hamburgers in London before returning home to the paternal vineyards and to advanced studies at the progressive teaching and experimentation estate in Montpellier, France. He introduced what he had learned there about pruning, grafting, pressing, and barrel construction over the objections of the other family members, who were content with the successes already achieved. Angelo began to produce single-vineyard barbarescos, first the Sori San Lorenzo, then Sori Gaja and Costa Russi. He supervised fermentation with temperature control—now done by computer. He experimented with *barriques,* and changed the pressing method to one that is extremely gentle, which naturally benefits the grappa pomaces. With these innovations he was soon creating world-class wines.

In 1978 Gaja again took a new tack and replaced the traditional barbera and dolcetto vines with cabernet sauvignon, chardonnay, and sauvignon blanc. His father's spontaneous "Darmagi!" (What a travesty!) gave the first product of the new vines its attention-getting name. The estate Darmagi, produced with the application of all the newest technical tricks, is an enormously concentrated wine full of fruit and incredible elegance. The Gaja & Rey, a single-variety chardonnay, also takes on a fruity sourness thanks to careful handling in the pressing. It is the product of longer fermentation in the mash, the use of wild yeasts instead of artificially grown fermenting agents, and fermentation on the sediment. These unconventional and advanced pressing techniques also benefit Gaja's grappas.

Grappa di Costa Russi

A grappa from the very moist pomaces of the single-vineyard Barbaresco Costa Russi, distilled immediately after racking in pot stills at the Distilleria del Barbaresco. Bottled after aging in the barrel at 90 proof (70 cl).

Very dark, honey-colored distillate with highly concentrated tones of wood and ripeness in its strong bouquet. The aroma is reminiscent of an ancient cupboard opened only after a long time: resin, raisins, dried herbs, a breath of camphor. In taste a heavy, concentrated sweetness with accentuated wood tannins, fruity and bitter in finish.

In its overall impression more in the line of a cognac than a grappa, but perfectly balanced between strength and elegance. A highly unusual digestive.

Additional Grappa
Vignarey

GIRARDI

VILLA GIRARDI
LOCALITÀ SAN PIETRO INCARIANO
37029 VERONA, VENETO

A thirty-four-hectare (eighty-four-acre) estate near Verona whose vineyards are distributed over three areas with protected origin designation: Bardolino, Soave, and Valpolicella. In addition to the dry wines of this region, it also produces traditional recioto and amarone from healthy corvina, rondinella, and molinara grapes air dried for months and therefore highly concentrated. The recioto is a botrytis-sweet, heavy dessert wine, the amarone a fully fermented, strong red wine with pleasantly astringent fruit tannins.

GRAPPA DI AMARONE DELLA VALPOLICELLA

From the mixed pomace of the Amarone della Valpolicella from the vineyard Opere di San Pietro from San Pietro Incariano. The pomace is fermented with the must, distilled in the traditional manner, and aged in small oak barrels (86 proof, 50 cl).

🍸 *Amber colored, with a distinctly nutty aroma; a soft, winy body; and a fruity finish.*

Additional Grappa
GRAPPA DI RECIOTO DELLA VALPOLICELLA

LA GIUSTINIANA

--◦--

**La Giustiniana
Rovereto di Gavi
15066 Alessandria, Piedmont**

One of the many imposing wine estates purchased by industrialists as either a hobby or a tax write-off. In this instance, that is a definite plus, yielding enough capital for investments in vineyards, cellars, and quality paired with an eye for marketing needs, all of which have made the wines of La Giustiniana into trendsetters. Especially the gavi: blond, sveldt, with mellow acid, an ideal accompaniment to today's lighter fish dishes. No wonder, for the small winegrowing region lies on the south edge of the Piedmont, almost in Liguria. Enrico Tomalino, the wine maker at La Giustiniana, produces wines suited to high-quality Mediterranean fish cuisine; in addition to the three single-site gavis Lugara, Centurionetta, and Montessora, there is a strong Gavi di Gavi fermented with the skins and aged in wood barrels.

The pomaces for the house grappa come exclusively from the Centurionetta vineyard and are fermented with the must.

Grappa di Gavi (1990)

Distilled on November 12, 1990, by Luigi Bossi in the copper still at Cunico in a limited edition of 4,442 bottles (84 proof, 50 cl).
Bottle no. 2,946: A warm, spicy grappa with a concentrated aroma of sweet fruit and fresh herbs, refreshing and invigorating on the palate, with pungent notes and a winy finish.

GRESY

Marchesi di Gresy
Tenute Cisa Asinara
12050 Barbaresco, Piedmont

*A*n estate founded in the last century by the marchesi of Gresy, but one whose winegrowing history can be traced back to Roman times. Alberto di Gresy has operated the estate for the past twenty years, assisted by cellar master Giuseppe Cortese. The wines of the best slopes, whose grapes have been coveted by top wine makers like Fontanafredda, can now mature into first-class vintages in the estate's own cellar. The grappas of the house are produced from the pomaces from various slopes.

Grappa di Nebbiolo Martinenga

Distilled in single batches using the vacuum method at the Distilleria del Barbaresco from the pomaces of the Barbaresco La Martinenga, fermented with the must and gently pressed (84 proof, 75 cl).

Refreshingly complex distillate with an outstanding development; strong aroma of nuts, chestnuts, mushrooms, roasted almonds, and caramel, with a fresh citrus tone; soft body and elegant finish.

Additional Grappas
Monte Aribaldo
Camp Gros
La Serra
Chardonnay

GREVEPESA

———◦———

CASTELLI DEL GREVEPESA
VIA GREVIGIANA, 34
50024 CASCIANO IN VAL DI PESA, TUSCANY

*I*t is unusual for a cooperative to enjoy an international reputation, to be considered one of the best wine producers in
Tuscany, and also to be a real pacemaker in the race for strict
quality controls. These 165 vintners from the Chianti Classico
region have willingly submitted to the strictest
controls for years now. They have been rewarded with success: on 650 hectares (1,606
acres) of DOCG slopes they produce first-class
vintage Chianti Classico and in addition some
single-vineyard Chiantis that are considered
among the elite wines of Italy. The vin santo is a
dessert wine rarity made from malvasia grapes
that are dried on straw mats from the time they
are harvested well into the winter—a process
that yields a concentrated must ideal for making
wines and grappas of very high quality.

AQUA ARDENS GRAPPA DI VIN SANTO

*Distilled slowly at Nannoni's and aged in the
small caratelli casks typically used for vin
santo. An amber-colored grappa rarity bottled at 84 proof in thin-walled 50 cl vials.*
  *An appetizingly spicy brandy with a
powerful aroma of almost overripe
fruit, surprisingly fresh in taste with a
pleasantly sweet finish.*

ISTITUTO AGRARIO DI SAN MICHELE

A AZIENDA AGRARIA DI ISTITUTO AGRARIO PROVINCIALE DI
SAN MICHELE ALL'ADIGE
VIA EDMONDO MACH, 1
38010 SAN MICHELE ALL'ADIGE, TRENTINO

*T*he internationally recognized winegrowing school of the Trentino, in which countless numbers of today's well-known vintners, enologists, cellar masters, and distillers received their training. The institute, established in a former Benedictine abbey in 1874, has served as the model for many other winegrowing schools around the world and, in addition to its research work, has made a name for itself with its wines, the sales of which support it.

The school's production of grappa is another branch of research, teaching, and financing. Distilling is accomplished in classic double-bottomed pot stills. Various methods are tested in the fermentation of pomaces, with each part distilled separately, and after scientific evaluation the results are blended into single-variety grappa *cuvées*.

GRAPPA DI VITIGNO MOSCATO

A strong grappa (90 proof, 50 cl) with a floral muscat bouquet, spicy taste notes, and a long, intense finish.

GRAPPA DI VITIGNO CHARDONNAY

An astonishingly successful grappa (90 proof, 50 cl) typical of the otherwise rather neutral chardonnay: fresh, with a strong grapy aroma, round body, and soft, lightly sweet finish.

Distillato di Uva Moscato Giallo

Distilled from whole fermented gold muscat grapes (88 proof, 50 cl). A harmonious brandy with a pleasantly spicy aroma, a flower-scented body, and delicate bitter tones.

Additional Grappas

Grappa di Schiava
Grappa di Cabernet
Grappa di Pinot Nero
Grappa di Müller-Thurgau
Grappa di Riesling R.
Grappa di Traminer
Grappa di Sauvignon

Acquavite d'Uva
Distillato Traminer

JERMANN

Azienda Agricola Vinnaioli Jermann
Località Villanova, Via Monte Fortino 21
34070 Farra d'Isonzo, Friuli

*O*ne of Silvio Jermann's chardonnay *cuvées* is called "Where the dreams have no end." That the Friulian wine maker still dreams more than twenty years after taking over the estate that has been in his family since 1881 is shown by his courage in creating new wines that again and again elicit astonishment and delight. With his multifaceted, original, and highly refined wines, Jermann is one of the top producers in Italy. He has not abandoned the old winegrowing tradition of the Friuli but has nevertheless overcome the limitations of the legally controlled designations. He also produces a strongly spicy tocai friulano, as well as picolit and ribolla gialla. The native Friuli varieties are not forgotten, only transformed into up-to-date modern wines full of character. His best wine at the moment is probably his *cuvée* Vintage Tunina, from sauvignon blanc, chardonnay, ribolla gialla, malvasia istriana, and picolit—a glowing, straw yellow delight with a strong aroma and balanced structure. From the pomaces of this *cuvée* he makes the grappa Spirt di Tunina, which offers no cause for complaint other than its scarcity. It was to be expected that Jermann would not be content with just a single grappa, it was to be hoped that his grappas would achieve the quality of his wines, and it was to be feared that they would be problematic. That we nevertheless count Jermann's grappas among our personal favorites shows once again how well he manages to merge his own desires with those of his friends. Quality has its own aroma, and here it is unmistakable.

GRAPPA JERMANN

A grappa from mixed pomaces of Jermann wines distilled twice in the traditional manner at Comar's in Aquileia and aged in oak barrels (90 proof, 70 cl).

A straw blond, highly successful distillate with an appetizing, fruity aroma that becomes richer and more voluminous as it develops in the glass. The first sip almost frightens with its aggressiveness, which rapidly softens and becomes increasingly harmonious well into the long, solid, but gentle finish. A real character!

GRAPPA SPIRT DI TUNINA

Distilled twice from pomaces of the Tunina cuvée (100 proof, 50 cl).

A clearly structured, more rustic distillate with a long-missed heartiness reminiscent of the "good old days" and of very high quality. Juicy, oily, nutty nose; powerful aroma; and gentle, nut-dominated development well into the delicately bitter finish—a grappa not easily forgotten.

Additional Grappa
SPIRT DI BELLINA

LEONE DE CASTRIS

——◦◦——

Azienda Agricola Vitivinicola Leone de Castris
Via Senatore de Castris 50
73015 Salice Salentino, Apulia

*T*he wine estate belonging to the noble Leone de Castris family was established in Salice Salentino in southern Apulia around the year 1600. The noble winegrowers rapidly acquired a good reputation and became established among producers for the courts of numerous Italian principalities—even popes were among their satisfied customers. In 1925 Leone de Castris presented the first rosé of its growing area, which quickly made a name for itself. Later renamed Five Roses, it continues to be an interesting wine and is one of the classics of this often underrated region. Today Salvatore Leone de Castris concentrates on producing up-to-date, strong, but not overpowering red wines that he presses in his ultramodern cellar, where he is happy to entertain visitors. The acquavite d'uva of the house is produced from the pomaces of the Five Roses.

Acquavite d'Uva Five Roses

Distilled twice in single batches with steam at Bonollo's from pomaces of the Five Roses rosé (80 proof, 50 cl).
A clear, fruity brandy with delicate floral overtones; strong but soft on the palate, with a long finish.

LIBRANDI

◦•◦

Azienda Vinicola Librandi
Cirò Marina, Strada Statale 106
Contrada San Gennaro
88072 Cirò Marina, Calabria

he estate of Antonio and Nicodemo Cataldo Librandi, established in 1940, is a model of forward-looking winegrowing in Calabria. After thorough modernization in the cellar and the vineyards, the Librandi brothers and their enologist Severino Garofano are now in a position to make wines of a high caliber. Despite the warm climate in the south of Italy, sauvignon blanc and chardonnay produce fresh, fruity, spritzig white wines; the gravello, made from cabernet sauvignon and the native gaglioppo vine, is one of the best red wines of southern Italy. The pride of the estate are its Cirò red wines, full of tradition yet lively and modern.

Torre Brezia

A grappa from the gaglioppo pomaces of the red wine Cirò, distilled twice at Comar's in Aquileia (86 proof, 75 cl).

Calabria's gentle side: a silver blond, very fruity, and well-rounded brandy with a number of associations with summer fruits. Soft on the palate, full of body, almost oily, with a respectable development of strength and a lovely resolution.

LUNGAROTTI

CANTINE LUNGAROTTI
VIA MARIO ANGELONI, 16
06089 TORGIANO, UMBRIA

Paterno

iorgio Lungarotti is one of the most original wine-making experts in Italy. His ideas and his modern vineyard have certainly changed wine making in Torgiano, even all of Umbria, helping to pave the way for very precisely controlled and guaranteed origin designations—which, though important historically, had lagged behind considerably in the wine making of this century—and elevating his region to new esteem. On his own estate Lungarotti produces chardonnays and cabernets in addition to the traditional vine varieties, experiments successfully with *cuvées,* and produces a dry aperitif, Solleone, reminiscent of sherry.

GRAPPA DI RUBESCO

From a mixed pomace of canaiolo and sangiovese from the Torgiano region fermented with the must and distilled in pot stills immediately after racking at Bonollo's. After the prescribed aging, bottled at 90 proof in 70 cl bottles; the label is adorned with a painting by the Baroque master Salvator Rosa (1615–1673).
A first-class grappa with a distinct personality: a masculine aroma of sandalwood, cinnamon, cloves, spices, musk, violets; in taste a gentle thrust of strength with complex bitter notes that echo delightfully for a long time.

MACULAN

—◇—

Azienda Agricola Maculan
Via Castelletto, 3
36042 Breganze, Veneto

B *arrique* aging takes skill. And skill comes from experimentation, study, and long reflection on vine varieties and wine making. Franco Maculan, one of the pioneers of the *barrique* movement, was already experimenting with them in the late 1970s. In his vineyards Maculan has relied on the familiar vine varieties of the Veneto: vespaiolo, the pinot family, the red cabernets, a little tocai, and Riesling. The only new variety he planted was chardonnay. Slow drying of healthy grapes, with the resulting concentration of fruit sugars and extracts, helps (when necessary) to improve the structure.

Grappa di Palazzotto (1994)

From gently pressed cabernet sauvignon pomaces of the red wine palazzotto, which is developed in barriques. *Distilled as soon as possible after racking at Poli's in Schiavon in traditional copper pot stills and aged in barriques on the estate (86 proof, total production 984 bottles, 70 cl).*

🍷 *Our sample no. 356: Amber colored, winy, spicy aroma with fresh grassy notes; voluminous in taste, with striking secondary aromas and an intense finish. Magnificent.*

MANZONI

Rocche dei Manzoni
Manzoni Soprani, 3
12665 Monforte d'Alba, Piedmont

More than almost any other Piedmont vintner, Valentino Migliorini was virtually predestined to produce first-class grappas. Before he turned to wine making he had owned a highly decorated restaurant in Piacenza, where he introduced his discriminating diners to the pleasures of the onetime poor people's brandy.

The wines of his fifty-hectare (124-acre) estate in the hills of Monforte d'Alba are delicate and refined. The vineyard's superb location is not the only reason. Migliorini has reduced the yield per hectare to at most 30 or 40 hectoliters (106 or 141 cubic feet) instead of the 60 (212) permitted by law. After fermentation he ages his wines in oak *barriques* with a capacity of 225 liters (59½ gallons). He finds that they acquire more color and vitality in such casks, the primary aromas of the wine blending harmoniously with the secondary ones from the barrel. *Barrique* aging is difficult, but Migliorini has plenty of experience; more than fifteen years ago he pioneered the revival of the old Piedmont tradition.

In addition to traditional single-variety wines such as his highly distinctive Dolcetto d'Alba, his internationally famous barolos from the vineyards d'la Roul (Piedmontese for oak) and Mosconi di Monforte, and his innovative Pinònero (from pinot noir vines) and chardonnay, Migliori produces a remarkable *cuvée* of 80 percent nebbiolo and 20 percent barbera: Bricco Manzoni. The dense fullness of the nebbiolo combines harmoniously with the fresh fruitiness of the barbera, and an aromatic sweetness and hints of vanilla are added as it ages in the barrel. Migliorini has managed to give some of the same flavor nuances to his Grappa di Bricco Manzoni.

Grappa di Bricco Manzoni

From the fermented pomaces of the top-quality Bricco Manzoni
cuvée. Golden yellow in color from barrique aging, bottled in ele-
gant vials (90 proof, 50 cl).

A strong distillate with a spicy aroma reminiscent of autumn
winds and overripe pumpkin; pleasant round body with hints
of phenol, a muted, ripe sweetness, and harmonious wood notes.

Grappa di Barolo

From the fermented nebbiolo pomaces of the barolos Vigna Big,
Vigna Mesdi, and Vigna d'la Roul. Distilled in Alba (100 proof,
50 cl).

A fresh, clear grappa with an almost ethe-
real barolo aroma, hints of medicinal
herbs, grass, hay, and spices. Reminiscent of a
lush green meadow in spring. The aromatic
components continue to be
harmonious but intensified
on the palate well into the
strong, vibrant finish.

MASI

——◦——

MASI AGRICOLA S.P.A.
LOCALITÀ GARGAGNANO
37020 S. AMBROGIO DI VALPOLICELLA, VENETO

*A*n ancient estate. The Boscaini family has been producing wine successfully in the Masi Valley since 1727. Two projects have assured it a head start in the Verona region. One was its identification and enclosure of historic slopes that from long experience and tradition are considered the best vineyards. The other was its dedication to the region's indigenous vine varieties, which thanks to deliberate reverse breeding have again yielded first-class wines. In addition to its high-quality bardolinos, valpolicellas, and soaves, the recione and amarone pressings from healthy corvina, rondinella, and molinara grapes that have been air dried for months are especially impressive, and it is these that provide the pomaces for the house grappa.

GRAPPA DI RECIOTO MEZZANELLA

From fresh moist pomaces of recioto from the Mezzanella vineyard in a small valley near Torbe; distilled in traditional pot stills and aged at least three years in 500-liter (132-gallon) barrels of Slovenian oak (100 proof, 50 cl).

A deep golden tone and a spicy, fresh aroma. Multilayered flavor with well-integrated wood aromas that develop enormous strength. Toasted aromas in the finish, which becomes more stringent but harmonious.

MASTROBERARDINO

AZIENDA VINICOLA MICHELE MASTROBERARDINO
VIA MANFREDI, 89
80342 ATRIPALDA, CAMPANIA

The Mastroberardino brothers' 130-hectare (321-acre) estate is one of the few rays of light in the wine-growing of this region. Antonio, the wine maker of the family, proves year after year how well suited the Campania's soils and sunny climate are to the production of top-quality wines, if only the vintner does his share. His formula: yield reduction, modern pressing techniques, and careful aging of the red wines in medium-sized barrels of Slovenian oak. His top product is the single-vineyard aglianico Taurasi Radici, which experts prophecy will keep for from fifty to sixty years.

GRAPPA NOVIA DI GRECO DI TUFO

A single-variety grappa from greco di tufo pomaces distilled in the Distilleria Aquileia di Comar in a double-bottomed still (80 proof, 70 cl).

🍷 *An unobtrusive aroma with delicate notes of grapefruit and hay and faint animal overtones; soft, winy taste.*

Additional Grappas
FIANO DI AVELLINO
AGLIANICO
CODADIVOLPE

MASTROIANNI

————◦————

Azienda Agraria Mastroianni
Castelnuove dell'Abate
53024 Montalcino, Tuscany

*I*n a wine landscape as booming as that of Tuscany it is not always easy to track down the producers who press truly great wines. Sudden demand attracts capital too quickly, people invest too much, plant too much, produce too much, and throw the wine on the market. The resurrected reputation of Brunello di Montalcino, for example, has led to a run on vineyards and estates around this small town in the province of Siena. One of the smaller, lesser-known, but very good estates is Mastroianni. With careful vine tending and pressing techniques and above all an independent notion of what brunello and its younger brother Rosso di Montalcino ought to be, it produces high-quality vintages full of character.

Grappa di Brunello di Montalcino

The still-moist pomaces are distilled immediately after racking in small pot stills at Nannoni's and aged in wooden barrels (86 proof, 50 cl).

A fully matured distillate with a lovely golden tone, hints of lemon peel and grapefruit in its aroma that develop into lemonade and orangeade on the palate; round, soft, with an earthy bittersweetness; a very complex brandy.

MEZZOCORONA

CANTINA SOCIALE COOPERATIVA DI MEZZOCORONA
LOCALITÀ MEZZOCORONA
38016 TRENTO, TRENTINO

A cooperative whose wines are prized internationally. Huge investments in pressing techniques and effective supervision of its members in the vineyard have made possible the production of wines that conform to the most modern notions without wholly abandoning tradition.

In addition to its fashionable chardonnay, the traditional teroldego vine plays a large role. The Teroldego Rotaliano made from it, with its own *denominazione,* is mild and full-bodied, with a breath of bittersweet. From its pomaces comes a grappa distilled under the personal supervision of the cooperative's technical director.

GRAPPA DI TEROLDEGO ROTALIANO (1990)

Distilled in traditional pot stills in a limited quantity of 15,300 bottles from pomaces of the red teroldego grape at the Distilleria Fedrizzi Toss (86 proof, 75 cl).

A harmonious, ingratiating brandy; reserved, elegant aroma with a breath of banana; a floral sweetness on the palate that develops into an intensely flowery finish.

MIONETTO

MIONETTO SPUMANTI S.R.L.
VIA COLDEROVE, 2
31049 VALDOBBIADENE, VENETO

*T*he fertile vineyards of the Veneto stretch from the shores of Venice's lagoon to the steep slopes of the Dolomites, through what was once called Terra Ferma, the Serenissima's rich hinterland. This is the home of the delicately yeasty prosecco vine and the spumante pressed from it. The best vineyard locations are in the rolling hills between Conegliano and Valdobbiadene, at the foot of the Maritime Alps.

Francesco Mionetto established his winery in Valdobbiadene in 1887 and acquired outstanding parcels not only there but also in the area around Cartizze and in the Euganean Hills, with their volcanic soils and warm microclimate. Today the estate also has vineyards in the valley of the Piave near Treviso, which are planted with pinot grigio, chardonnay, cabernet, and marzemino.

Chief enologist Sergio Mionetto uses the grapes grown there in the production of spumante. In addition to the traditional champagne method, Mionetto employs the Charmat technique typical of the region as well as Casada, the traditional method of neighboring Treviso—different production techniques for different characteristics. The classic Prosecco Legatura is one of the best-known examples of its type: vibrant straw yellow, with a slight effervescence and fruity bouquet, it displays the qualities with which sparkling wines from the prosecco vine—not all of them so flawless—have captured devoted fans. Mionetto does his best business in Venice itself. There it is still customary to stop in a small wine bar at eleven in the morning for an ombra, a small glass of fresh, slightly sparkling white wine from the region, preferably from Valdobbiadene. Mionetto's excellent reputation accounts for the popping of plenty of corks in the city on the lagoon.

No air is allowed to reach the pomaces from Mionetto's wines during fermentation, and immediately afterward they are distilled with steam in a traditional copper pot still. In this way he produces single-variety grappas that nicely round out his high-quality offerings.

Grappa di Prosecco di Valdobbiadene

Distilled twice in copper stills from prosecco pomaces from Valdobbiadene and harmonized in glass flasks (84 proof, 70 cl).

A winy distillate redolent of early autumn—hay, grasses, mushrooms, brushwood—and with a delicately spicy finish.

Vite di Cartizze

The distillate of prosecco pomaces from Cartizze, the supreme Valdobbiadene location; distilled twice and harmonized in glass flasks (84 proof, 50 cl).

A cheerful summer grappa: lively aroma with delicate fruit and flower scents, on the palate a successful blend of flower and spice; complex finish.

Additional Grappas
Vite d'Uva
Vite di Prosecco e
  Cartizze
Grappa di Chardonnay
Grappa Casada
Vite di Prosecco

NITTARDI

Fattoria Nittardi
Castellina in Chianti
53011 Siena, Tuscany

*F*or Michelangelo, wines from Nittardi were the very best. Little wonder, for he owned this estate first documented in 1182. The present-day owners, Stefania Canali and her German husband, Peter Femfert, an art dealer, have been inspired by the *fattoria's* past artistic associations and turned the previously agricultural operation with its eight hectares (twenty acres) of vineyards, forest, and olive groves into a cultural center with a painting, language, and cooking school; comfortable guest apartments; and varied offerings for culture tourists.

But wine making is by no means neglected. Chianti Classico and the white Biondo di Nittardi from fashionable trebbiano and the related malvasia, known in antiquity, are produced in the strictly classic manner by enologist Carolo Ferrini. His heavy pruning, traditional pressing in old wooden presses, mash fermentation for the red wines, and aging in wood produce fine, appealing wines.

The Chianti Classico pomaces are distilled in the Nannoni distillery using a combination of continuous and discontinuous techniques.

Grappa di Chianti Classico (1991)

Limited to 1,016 bottles (84 proof, 75 cl).

Our sample no. 230: A mature grappa with perfectly integrated nutty aromas; a winy, substantial body; and a protracted finish.

Grappa di Chianti Classico (1992)

Limited edition of 3,700 bottles (84 proof, 75 cl).

Our sample no. 9: A complex distillate with a rich aroma; round, soft, voluminous, fruity, and nicely nutty; very harmonious taste and pleasant finish; winier than the previous year's.

ORNELLAIA

TENUTA DELL'ORNELLAIA
VIA BOLGHERESE, 191
57020 BOLGHERI, TUSCANY

This winery is owned by Marchese Lodovico Antinori, but is independent of the family business. The region of the Maremma, near the Tyrrhenian Sea, has only a brief wine-making tradition: in the mid-1970s, when his older brother Piero was setting the pace in the revival of Tuscany's wines, the world traveler and consultant Lodovico did not want to be left behind. He too had a vision of what red wine ought to be and sufficient capital to realize it despite all obstacles. On the Ornellaia estate, inherited from his mother, he hoped to plant vines from which he could make a great, full-bodied, long-lived red wine with a distinct character of its own. Soil tests were encouraging: the com-

Ornellaia, a hypermodern cantina

position was somewhat similar to that in California's Napa and Sonoma Valleys.

The ground was quickly cleared and planted with cabernet, merlot, sémillon, and sauvignon blanc. A hypermodern cellar was created and one of California's best enologists, André Tchelistcheff, was engaged. As cellar master, his pupil Federico Staderini ensures continuity at Ornellaia. The estate's showpiece, proudly called simply Ornellaia, contains 80 percent cabernet and 20 percent merlot. It is an intensely fruity wine with a complex aroma, a soft, almost velvety body, and harmoniously integrated tannins. In addition, the estate makes a single-variety merlot called Masseto, likewise aged in *barriques,* as well as the white wine based on the Bordelais model called Poggio alle Gazze.

GRAPPA DI MERLOT

A Nannoni distillate from fresh merlot pomaces that is aged in barriques until it has fully matured (84 proof, 50 cl).

A noble grappa that evokes preparations for Christmas: rich aromas of spices, cloves, vanilla, stewed fruit. A soft, warm body, with a long, harmonious finish.

Additional Grappa
GRAPPA DI CABERNET SAUVIGNON

IL PALAZZINO

Podere Il Palazzino
Località Monti
53010 Gaiole in Chianti, Tuscany

*A*lessandro and Andrea Sderci have owned this wine estate since 1972. They have chosen to concentrate on only a few varieties. A fortunate decision for wine lovers—the Chianti Classico Grosso Senese is one of the outstanding wines of the region, as professional tasters confirm. In a cozy room on the estate it is possible to taste both its wines and the charming grappa from pomaces of Chianti Classico. The prices of the Sderci wines have unfortunately risen to match those of neighboring estates, but they are worth every penny.

Grappa di Chianti Classico

Distilled twice in the traditional manner at the Giovi distillery in Sicily from pomaces of Chianti Classico, harmonized for a long period before bottling (87 proof, 50 cl).

A floral, spicy grappa that unleashes a real explosion of strength on the palate; a harmony of lighter and darker notes in its aroma up into the hearty, consistently masculine finish.

PAVESE

LIVIO PAVESE
TREVILLE-MONFERRATO
15030 ALESSANDRIA, PIEDMONT

*L*ivio Pavese is a modern wine maker from an old, established winegrowing family in Treville, in the Monferrato Hills north of Alessandria. His vineyard purchases, his deliberate yield reduction, his investments in up-to-date pressing techniques, and his successful experiments with *barrique* aging have helped to bring Pavese's wines international recognition. For his grappa, however, he relies on Piedmontese tradition: pomaces of native grape varieties are distilled the way his great-grandfather did it, with the results aged in large wooden barrels.

GRAPPA STRAVECCHIA DA VINACCE DEL MONFERRATO

From barbera pomaces to which a maximum of 15 percent freisa or grignolino has been added. Distilled in pot stills at the Distilleria Cooperativa Rosignanio and aged on the estate for more than twelve months in wooden barrels: first in 500-liter (132-gallon) casks, then, to intensify the aroma, in 220-liter (58-gallon) barriques (90 proof, 70 cl).

Straw blond in color, a straightforward aroma of herbs and spices, a robust but well-rounded body with a hint of medicinal herbs in its taste and softening finish. A good digestive with a slight Amaro quality.

PIETRAFITTA

Fattoria di Pietrafitta
San Gimignano
53037 Siena, Tuscany

The towers of San Gimignano soar high above the vineyards into the blue sky of Tuscany, visible from afar in every direction. More fortresses than dwellings, they stand as mute witnesses to a time when it was necessary to defend the community against bands of marauders and covetous princes.

The Vernaccia di San Gimignano can be grown only around this city between Florence and Siena. Traditionally, it is harvested late and transformed into a heavy, alcohol-rich wine through long fermentation on the pomace and aging in wooden barrels. Its modern version lacks the nobility and effervescence of other Tuscan white wines. At Pietrafitta they seek a compromise, producing contemporary wines that nevertheless have much of the traditional about them. The grappas distilled from their pomaces have a character all their own.

Grappa di Vernaccia di San Gimignano

Distilled in the traditional manner at Bonollo's (84 proof, 50 cl).

❦ *A very gentle brandy; at first its aroma is reserved, but soon ripe fruit and winy raisin notes develop. Simple but noble, a lovely grappa.*

PIGHIN

◦—◦—◦

Azienda Fratelli Pighin
Frazione Risano, Viale Gradi 1
33050 Pavia di Udine, Friuli

*T*he Pighin brothers' estate numbers among the solid producers of the region and is considered an example of how innovation can be successfully paired with respect for tradition. Still, one fears that the Pighins may try to enhance their image by raising the prices of their uncommonly reasonable wines. Their elegant white wines prove to be straightforward, respectable, and yet complex, just like their soft, highly aromatic red wines. But Pighin wines are still good choices for connoisseurs, and the same can be said of their successful grappa made from sauvignon blanc pomaces, which seldom produce such outstanding brandies.

Grappa di Sauvignon (1994)

A single-variety grappa from sauvignon blanc pomaces distilled in a limited edition of 15,000 bottles at Pagura in Castions di Zoppola (86 proof, 50 cl).

Our sample no. 10,732: A refreshing, light, and highly idiosyncratic distillate with grassy green nose. A delicate aroma with floral accents, a delightfully soft, fresh taste to the substance-rich, medium-heavy body, and a finish characterized by a delicate bitterness and peppery spice.

PISONI

Azienda Agricola e Distilleria Pisoni
Località Pergolese
38070 Sarche, Trentino

A winery and distillery with roots that reach back to the six-teenth century. The products from its copper still were prized by the archbishop of Trento as early as about 1730. Today Pisoni still produces the sacramental wines for the Trento bish-opric. Luca, Marco, and Stefano Pisoni, the present owners, have adopted their ancestor Baldessare's preferred methods, having new stills created after the pattern of his ancient *alambicco*. They have also expanded their production of first-class grappas.

Grappa Trentina Müller-Thurgau (1991)

Gently pressed then further fermented Thurgau pomaces from the Valle dei Laghi. First distilled over steam in a continuous still, then again in a small double-bottomed pot still at low temper-atures (86 proof, 50 cl).

A fragile power packet with a winy, nutty aroma, a soft body, and a harmonious finish that gains in sweetness.

Additional Grappas
Nosiola
Vecchia Riserva
Moscato
Schiava Gentile
Teroldego
Tipica Trentina

POGGIO ANTICO

—◦►—

Fattoria Poggio Antico
Località Poggio Antico
53024 Montalcino, Tuscany

𝒜 tradition-oriented, highly quality-conscious Tuscan estate. On its 200 hectares (494 acres) of vineyards—including 20 hectares (49 acres) in Montalcino's best brunello zone—they grow exclusively the classic sangiovese grosso vine, which they turn into brunello or Rosso di Montalcino. Owned by Milanese industrialists, the estate gave new impetus to the current debate about the regulations governing the production of brunello when it presented its vino da tavola Altero, a sangiovese wine from Montalcino with a noble, highly individual character and an elegant lightness. Brunello pomaces are used for the grappa of the house. The long fermentation in the mash of the heavier brunello makes for better grappa pomaces.

Grappa di Brunello

Distilled with steam at Nannoni's in stills of various sizes from very fresh pomaces of sangiovese grosso fermented with the mash. Aged in the distillery (85 proof, 70 cl).

▐ *A nutty grappa with a rich fruit: plums, apricots, and yellow plums prevail over a breath of bitter almond or acacia; a warm, mellow body with a soft, gentle finish.*

POJER & SANDRI

---◦---

AZIENDA AGRICOLA POJER & SANDRI
LOCALITÀ MOLINI
38010 FAEDO, TRENTINO

*I*s this a winery or a distillery? It is a question that Mario Pojer and Fiorentino Sandri never ask themselves. Dedicated wine makers, they also distill professionally in their own distillery. The two became partners twenty-five years ago when they were students at the wine-making school in San Michele all'Adige. It was for their wines that they became known, based on such innovative vine varieties as chardonnay, sauvignon, and Müller-Thurgau. By planting them garden style and fermenting them in such a way as to achieve the desired aroma, the two managed to produce racy but aromatic white wines and substantial rosés, vintages quite unheard of in their day but now characteristic of the internationally esteemed Trentino style. Their Chardonnay di Faedo is especially prized: when it appeared, the wine experts raved that it was impossible to imagine a better location for chardonnay than the Trentino—high praise, given the worldwide competition in wines from this fashionable grape. For some time the two partners have also been producing a highly aromatic and delicately effervescent spumante from the champagne vine varieties chardonnay and pinot noir, aging it on the yeast for several years.

They began making grappa at the start, but halted production in 1975, as it was too unprofitable to be worthwhile. In 1982 they took it up again on a larger scale, and by now they are producing some seven thousand bottles a year. With just one exception they use only their own pomaces, keeping them very moist and, if necessary, adding a dose of the pressing to achieve the tenderness that makes for good grappa.

GRAPPA MÜLLER-THURGAU (1990)

Distilled in a double-bottomed pot still from very moist pomaces (fermented in their own winery) of Müller-Thurgau from their own vines (96 proof, 70 cl).

A full, highly complex distillate with a heavy aroma of berries, nuts, and ripe fruit; gentle and round on the palate with winy notes and a breath of pepper in its fruity, ripe finish.

GRAPPA DI MOSCATO ROSA (1990)

Distilled in their own double-bottomed still from very moist pomaces of the rosé muscat from the winery of the Conti Kuenburg in Caldaro (96 proof, 50 cl).

A noble brandy with the typical floral nose of rosé muscat; deep spicy notes and ripe, very sweet fruit round out the aroma. In taste a spicy, bitter tone dominates, a pleasant contrast to the breath of potpourri. A long, consistent finish.

Additional Grappas

FRAGOLINO
CHARDONNAY
NOSIOLA
VIN DEI MOLINO

PUNSET

—◦—

AZIENDA AGRICOLA PUNSET
FRAZIONE MORETTA 42
12057 NEIVE, PIEDMONT

*T*he Punset family estate is one of the best operations in the wine village of Neive and is known to grappa lovers mainly as the home and workplace of the cult distiller Romano Levi (see pages 12–13). Though Levi's grappas vary widely, owing to his use of an antediluvian still, Punset's are perfectly reliable, as pure and aroma intensive as its wines, both of which can be sampled in a charming tasting room on the estate. Marina and Renzo Macarino are especially proud of their single-vineyard Barbera d'Alba from the vigneto zocco, but even the standard barbera disproves the notion that only rustic wines can be made from this variety. They also produce barbaresco, including the single-vineyard Barbaresco Campo Quadro, and Dolcetto d'Alba.

GRAPPA STRAVECCHIA DI MOSCATO

Distilled twice in the traditional manner and aged for three years in oak barrels, a single-variety grappa made from muscat grapes (84 proof, 70 cl).

🍷 *A light gold brandy with an aroma dominated by fruit and spice—licorice, pepper, Brazil nuts, oranges—and warm honey-syrup tones on the palate, with a note of piquancy in the long finish.*

LE PUPILLE

---◦►---

FATTORIA LE PUPILLE
LOCALITÀ PERETA
58051 MAGLIANO IN TOSCANA, TUSCANY

This estate in the foothills of the Maremma, not far from Grosseto, belongs to the dedicated wine maker Elisabetta Geppetti. For some years the Fattoria Le Pupille has occupied a top position in the area, impressing experts not only with its creative table wine *cuvées* but also with its Morellino di Scansano, a local DOC specialty that owes its rating to Geppetti. This wine, mostly sangiovese but with small additions of ciliegiolo, canaiolo, and alicante, is noted for its velvety softness and full aroma of late summer fruit, compote, and spicy pepper, features found also in the grappa distilled from the pomaces of this *cuvée*.

GRAPPA DELLE PUPILLE

Distilled in single batches with steam at the Distilleria Astigiana in Mombercelli from pomaces of the Tuscan specialty Morellino di Scansano (84 proof, 70 cl).

A lighthearted, gentle brandy with highly complex fruit and honey aromas offset by herbal and nutty notes. Its appetizing full flavor becomes somewhat drier in the multifaceted finish. A superb distillate.

RUGGERI

Ruggeri e C. s.p.a.
Via Garibaldi, 13
31049 Valdobbiadene, Veneto

A wine estate that has made a name for itself primarily with its production of spumante from the prosecco vine. But it also produces first-class single-vineyard spumantes from the *cru* Cartizze. In 1992 the operation revived an old tradition of the founding Bisol family: to commemorate the distillery of Eliseo Bisol, founded in Valdobbiadene in 1850, they produced two grappas from the prosecco and Cartizze Prosecco pomaces.

Grappa di Cartizze

Inspired by late summer delights, a stately grappa with a rich aroma of fruit and spices, round and gentle with a pleasantly long finish (84 proof, 50 cl).

Grappa di Prosecco

A somewhat reserved distillate that hides its ripe fruit notes behind sorrel and hay aromas; sweetish and round on the palate with a finish that is biting at first but then grows warmer (84 proof, 50 cl).

SAN GUIDO

❧◦❧

TENUTA SAN GUIDO
LOCALITÀ CAPANNE 27
57020 BOLGHERI, TUSCANY

*T*he Tenuta San Guido, established by Marchese Nicolò Incisa della Rocchetta in 1968, is one of the most famous wine estates in Italy. This is chiefly owing to the red wine *cuvée* produced here from 85 percent cabernet sauvignon and 15 percent cabernet franc. At the beginning only 3,000 bottles were produced a year, but the wine soon achieved cult status. By now, production is at more than 100,000 bottles. Recently the vineyard sites Castiglioncello, Sassicaia, and Alanova, all wholly owned by Incisa, were granted DOC status. Another recent development: the estate's pomaces are now distilled at Jacopo Poli's, guaranteeing high quality for the Grappa di Sassicaia.

GRAPPA DA VINACCE DI SASSICAIA

Distilled with steam in single batches from pomaces of the red wine cuvée *Sassicaia and aged in barriques (80 proof, 50 cl).*

An amber-colored, warm, and spicy distillate with an abundance of pre-Christmas notes—marzipan, dried fruits, citron, cinnamon—that are set off by a rather deep grassy freshness. The consistent development and expansion of the aroma structure on the palate and in the finish underscore the refinement and elegance of this complex brandy.

SAN MICHELE

❖

Podere San Michele
Harald L. Bremer
Via della Beccaccia, 1
58043 Castiglione della Pescaia, Tuscany

*I*t was only logical that the multitalented wine lover, wine dealer, and glass designer Harald L. Bremer from Brunswick, Germany, would become a wine maker as well. His offerings include a lovely selection of Tuscan wines, and his grappa selection is equally well considered. After countless tastings and active investigation of the winegrowing culture of this central Italian landscape, he finally bought a vineyard. Success came in his first year. The wine called Vetluna from his Podere San Michele in Vetulonia has been one of the top offerings from his varied catalog for several years now. Since 1988 Bremer has been using the distiller Gioacchino Nannoni in Paganico, only half an hour away, sending him a mixture of very moist, essentially unpressed pomaces and whole Vetluna grapes.

Grappa delle Vinacce di Vetluna (1991)

A grappa aged for thirty months in barriques *made of French Nevers oak (94 proof, 75 cl).*

🍷 *An enchanting brandy with tart citrus aromas on top of a ripe fruitiness that continues in the full body and into the warm but refreshing finish.*

SAN VITO

**Tenuta San Vito in Fior di Selva
Via San Vito, 32
50065 Montelupo Fiorentino, Tuscany**

A family estate in the Florentine hills of Tuscany with twenty-six hectares (sixty-four acres) of vineyards. Owner Roberto Drighi and his daughter Laura, who oversees the operation, have committed themselves to ecological wine making. Since 1981 the products of the winery have been made using organic methods; their quality is checked by the Associazone Italiana Agricoltura Biologica and guaranteed by the seal "Garanzia A.I.A.B." Needless to say, the grappa of the house is also made from ecologically produced Chianti pomaces.

Grappa Fior di Selva

Distilled at low temperatures in the steam-heated Calderini still at the Nannoni distillery in Paganico within forty-eight hours of racking (84 proof, 50 cl).

An exquisite brandy with an intense, complex, nutty aroma, spicy and dense; a firm, substantial body and a soft and long-lasting finish. A consistent grappa with harmonious structure.

Additional Grappa

Grappa Riserva, *aged in oak for a year*

SANTA MARGHERITA

Santa Margherita
Fossalta di Portogruaro
30025 Venice, Veneto

To wine guru Hugh Johnson, the estate belonging to the counts of Marzotto is "indisputably Italy's leader in pinot grigio." According to the English connoisseur, the "avant-gardist" estate has made a name for itself with its young, acidic wines in the modern mode. Not relying only on such fashionable vines as chardonnay and pinot, the cellar master Giorgio Mascarin also develops the venerable tocai of the Lison-Pramaggiore region into a lean, simple wine. Innovation is indeed a tradition at Santa Margherita. As for its grape brandies, it produces not only a grappa but also a *distillato d'uva*—a traditional product that was made in the eastern Veneto between Trieste and Venice as early as the twelfth century.

Santa Margherita Distillato d'Uva Pinot Grigio

From the whole grapes of pinot grigio, which ferment for eight to ten days in small, temperature-controlled tanks before being distilled in a vacuum in modern copper stills (80 proof, 70 cl).

A discreet brandy with an unimposing aroma with delicate hints of citrus; winy body, elegant bitter notes.

VINI SCOPETANI

**Fattoria Il Frantoio
Località Rufina
50068 Florence, Tuscany**

*T*he wine dealer Guido Scopetani acquired this *fattoria* in the first-class Chianti region of Rufina some years ago so he would no longer have to be dependent on contract wine makers in his quest for better wines. Extensive investments in the vineyards and cellars have led to the desired result: lovely Chianti Rufina, from whose pomaces, fermented with the must, is distilled a brandy of high quality called Grappola.

"Grappola"—Grappa di Chianti Rufina

Distilled in pot stills at Bonollo's in Greve in Chianti and bottled at 84 proof in slender black 50 cl bottles.

A gentle, warm grappa with a lovely aroma of mushrooms, spices, and fruit, round and grapy on the palate with bitter almond in the finish. An exquisite brandy.

SELLA & MOSCA

Tenute Sella & Mosca
Località I Piani
07041, Alghero, Sardinia

In 1899 the engineer Emilio Sella and the jurist Edgardo Mosca turned their backs on their Piedmontese homeland and settled in the interior of Sardinia. Their winery rapidly became one of the most important producers on the island, which has a wealth of indigenous vine varieties matched by scarcely any other region. The wines of Sella & Mosca—whether their Monica di Sardegna, Cannonau di Alghero, Torbato, Nasco di Cagliari, or Vermentino—offer a good introduction to Sardinia's traditional vine varieties. Modern *cuvées* like their Tanca Farrà and Oleandro are up-to-date counterparts. Their most original product is the red dessert wine Anghelu Ruju, made from sun-dried cannonau grapes. After aging for years in the barrel it still has to mature in the bottle, much like port. The house grappa is distilled from the fermented pomaces of these grapes rich in sugars and extracts.

Grappa Anghelu Ruju

Distilled in traditional pot stills and bottled in tall, slender bottles after the prescribed aging (84 proof, 50 cl).

 A very expressive grappa with a summery, fruity aroma of berries and flowers, a soft, rather bright body, and a strong finish with floral elements.

Winegrowing in Sardinia

TASCA D'ALMERITA

―◦―

Tenuta Regaleali di Conte Tasca d'Almerita
Località Regaleali
90020 Sclafani Bagni, Sicily

*H*ere the butler makes the wine, an indication of both the democratic instincts of the estate's owner, Conte Giuseppe Tasca d'Almerita, and the great knowledge and organizational skills acquired through the years by the former majordomo Curcio, which now benefit the entire estate. The count also demonstrates his independence by forgoing DOC wines: his first-class products from various varieties of grapes are marketed simply as Rosso del Conte or Regaleali Bianco, Rosato, or Rosso. Critics and wine lovers have never let that deter them—the count's vintages have long enjoyed cult status. Notable examples are his 1990 Regaleali Chardonnay and his Nozze d'Oro, a *cuvée* of sauvignon blanc and the sauterne variant inzoli that has been produced each year since the count and countess celebrated their golden wedding anniversary in 1984.

Here they are always open to innovation. The two hundred hectares (494 acres) of vineyards have been converted to trellis growth, which in the hot climate of Sicily helps ensure healthy grapes. In addition to the traditional Sicilian vine varieties there are plantings of sauvignon blanc and cabernet sauvignon that thrive in the chalky clay soil.

They are also using new methods in the redesigned cellar. The Rosso del Conte, from perricone and nero d'Avola vines, a classic Sicilian wine only rarely blessed with top quality, is now matured in oak *barriques* instead of chestnut barrels—with outstanding success. Its pomaces, fermented with the must like those of the single-variety chardonnay, are turned into grappa at the famous Giovi distillery.

Grappa di Rosso del Conte

Pomaces from the vine varieties nero d'Avola and perricone; distilled in single batches in double-bottomed pot stills (86 proof, 50 cl).

🍷 A radiant, light distillate with a complex aroma of flowers and grapes, a supple body with a definite harmony between strength and reserve, and a delicate finish with lovely bitter notes. A masculine brandy full of elegance.

Grappa di Chardonnay

From pomaces from the estate's own chardonnay vineyards, which are fermented after pressing under controlled temperatures. Once fermentation is complete, they are immediately distilled in double-bottomed pot stills at the Giovi distillery. Bottled in the distillery at 86 proof (50 cl).

🍷 A somewhat one-dimensional but good-quality grappa with a clean bouquet, a fresh body, and a bittersweet finish.

TEDESCHI

◦

Fratelli Tedeschi
Via Verdi, 4
37020 S. Pietro in Cariano/Pedemonte, Veneto

*I*n the last twenty years the brothers Renzo and Silvino Tedeschi have cautiously modernized the methods of their ancestors, who began making wine here in 1884. They have adopted modern pressing techniques without changing the types of wines they make. In addition to outstanding valpolicellas they now produce the single-vineyard Valpolicella Capitel San Rocco delle Lucchine. They still hold to the venerable recioto and amarone versions of valpolicella: select, healthy grapes are carefully dried after harvest until Christmas in order to raise their concentration of extracts and fruit sugars. The deliberately slow fermentation is interrupted for the botrytis-sweet recioto; the full-bodied, tannin rich, but velvety amarone is fully fermented and dry.

Grappa Capitel

Distilled by Bruno Franceschini from fermented recioto pomaces from the vineyards of Monte Fontana and Monte Olmi and aged in oak barrels (90 proof, 70 cl).

Light amber in color, fully ripened aroma with distinct secondary aromas, deep taste with slightly biting finish that develops into a grapy sweetness. Definitely a digestive grappa, perfect after dessert.

TERRABIANCA

AZIENDA TERRABIANCA
RADDA IN CHIANTI
53017 SIENA, TUSCANY

For some years now the once famous but subsequently abandoned and run-down properties of Tuscany have become collectors' items for successful entrepreneurs eager to fulfill their dreams of country life as wine makers in the heart of the Chianti region. With his purchase of Terrabianca, the Zurich fashion maven Roberto Guldener was hoping for a new challenge, and in the experienced advisor Vittorio Fiore he found a like-minded wine maker who could carry out his plans.

Organic fertilization, rigorous yield reduction, and selective harvest by hand ensure healthy grapes. Temperature-controlled fermentation and aging in *barriques* of oak from Alliers, the Troncais, or the Vosges, as well as in larger oak barrels, make for top-quality wines—elegant, well structured, and durable.

GRAPPA LA BOMBA

Distilled twice in steam alembics at the Bonollo distillery in Formigine (90 proof, 70 cl)

An elegant brandy with a rich, grapy aroma and a rather sweet taste, with an almost liqueurlike finish.

TERRE DA VINO

LE AZIENDE AGRICOLE DI TERRE DA VINO
VIA ROMA, 50
10020 MORIONDO, PIEDMONT

A winery and sales cooperative founded in 1980 and made up of the Piedmontese estates Cascine dell'Aureliana, Masseria dei Carmelitani, Tenuta Cannona, San Nicolao, Roccabella, La Villa, Baiarda, Brichet, Poderi Parussi, Vezzolano, and Bricco del Bosco. In addition to the members' wines it also markets its own high-quality wine from the growing zones Barbera d'Asti, Barolo, and Barbaresco.

The winery's grappas are single varieties, distilled from pomaces of various estates.

GRAPPA DI NEBBIOLO DA BAROLO

Distilled in copper stills immediately after the racking of the fermented Barolo must (90 proof, 50 cl).

Scents of an autumn day in the Piedmont—mushrooms, nuts, herbs, grapes, currants, and blackberries—in the very dense aroma, which is followed by an intense harmony of bitter chocolate and wine.

Grappa di Cortese di Gavi

Distilled in steam-heated copper stills immediately after fermentation from pomaces of the white cortese from the Gavi region at the Antica Distilleria Quaglia (90 proof, 50 cl).

❦ *A refreshing white wine grappa with a vibrant nose—nuts, sorrel—and a powerful body; substantial, firm, dense; an explosion of aroma in the long finish.*

The idyllic Terre da Vino headquarters

TIGLIO

---◦►---

Azienda Agricola Borgo del Tiglio
Via San Giorgio, 71
34070 Brazzano di Cormons, Friuli

*A*t his model small winery Nicola Manferrari produces only about 25,000 bottles a year. They are some of the best wines of the Friuli, even though Manferrari resists the current trend of his region—light, fashionable wines are not his interest. The few hectares belonging to the family business, which he took over in 1981, are planted, as always, with the traditional vine varieties of the Collio region: tocai, merlot, and malvasia. Only in recent years has he added a little chardonnay. With a successful synthesis of traditional methods and the most modern pressing technique, the forward-looking wine maker has positioned himself for the production of fruity, aroma-intensive, and long-lived wines—even the chardonnay.

Borgo del Tiglio

A Nannoni grappa from white pomaces distilled at low temperatures in the combined continuous/discontinuous technique (84 proof, 75 cl).

A reserved aroma with delicate nut and rose scents, a vibrant body with harmonious grass tones in the intense, tingling finish.

VENEGAZZÙ

**VENEGAZZÙ-CONTE LOREDAN-GASPARINI
VIA MARTIGNANO ALTO, 24
31040 VENEGAZZÙ DEL MONTELLO, VENETO**

noble estate and a leader in the adoption of the *barrique* in Italy. It also produces good spumante and prosecco-frizzante.

GRAPPA RIVA VECIA

Pinot, cabernet, and prosecco pomaces distilled twice in pot stills (86 proof, 70 cl).

🍷 *A fresh, fruity bouquet of cherries, berries, bitter almond; bittersweet finish.*

GRAPPA DI PROSECCO RISERVA

Distilled twice in pot stills and aged for more than a year in small oak barrels (80 proof, 70 cl).

🍷 *Light gold, well rounded, with appetizing fruit aromas; aromatic and delicate on the palate—spice tones, restrained secondary aromas; lovely finish that grows warmer.*

VERRAZZANO

Castello di Verrazzano
Località Greti
50022 Greve in Chianti, Tuscany

*A*n up-and-coming estate in an old, massive fortress, at one time a refuge for the Florentine aristocracy and its serfs. They have been making wine here since 1170. The *castello,* high above the meandering Greve in the north of the Chianti region, is surrounded by forty hectares (ninety-nine acres) of vineyards planted mainly with sangiovese for use in Chianti Classico. Deliberately small yields, harvesting in several different stages, and short delivery routes make possible the production of fine Chiantis and Riservas. Also rooted in the old traditions is its production of vin santo from dried, botrytis-sweetened grapes. On the other hand, its vini da tavola Sasello and Bottiglia Particolare, made from 80 percent sangiovese and 20 percent cabernet, are altogether modern in style.

Grappa di Castello di Verrazzano (1989)

Fresh, moist mixed pomaces distilled three times with steam at Nannoni's in stills of decreasing size. After six months of tank aging, bottled at 86 proof in 6,050 numbered 50 cl bottles.

Our sample no. 1,495: A complex brandy with a winy aroma, fruity hints of pears and apples, a full body, and vibrant finish.

VICCHIOMAGGIO

TENUTA DI VICCHIOMAGGIO
VIA VICCHIOMAGGIO, 4
50022 GREVE IN CHIANTI, TUSCANY

*O*ne of the loveliest estates in Tuscany. The Castello di Vicchiomaggio dates back more than a thousand years. First mentioned in 957, the prominent fortress was acquired in the early 1960s by the Englishman John Matta. He produced his first wine only in 1964, and currently he has roughly twenty-five hectares (sixty-two acres) of vineyards. It was no simple undertaking to produce first-class wines in such a relatively short time; a thorough study of the soil and microclimate helped. Depending on conditions, he planted the various vine varieties used in the Chianti Classico *cuvée,* and the resulting, well-structured wines are celebrated for their fascinating softness. The grappa of the house, distilled at the Nannoni distillery, is made from a mixture of pomaces from various locations.

GRAPPA CASTELLO VICCHIOMAGGIO

Distilled three times in pot stills (84 proof, 1 liter; our sample bottle unfortunately had a crumbling cork).

A heavy bouquet with rich offerings of Russian leather and heavy citrus tones such as grapefruit and orange; becomes somewhat lighter on the palate with a winy, slightly aggressive finish.

VIETTI

———◦▸———

VIETTI
PIAZZA VITTORIO VENETO, 5
12060 CASTIGLIONE FALLETTO, PIEDMONT

A winery and a cantina in one. Like almost no one else, Alfredo Currado has managed to capitalize on the long-standing contacts of his house with the owners of the best slopes in the Piedmont and to produce superb wines from purchased grapes as well as those from his own harvest. Along with his son-in-law Mario Cordero, he is one of the Piedmont's pioneers. Through skillful application of the most modern pressing techniques, despite their use of traditional wood barrels, they have managed to eliminate the oxidation and weakness of the barolo that were long held to be typical of even the best Piedmontese wines. Temperature-controlled fermentation tanks stand next to well-maintained, venerable barrels of Slovenian oak. To be sure, the house has also begun experimenting with *barriques* of French oak, and the wines currently offered are modern classics, a compromise between historic splendor and modern elegance achieved by hard work, long experience, and determination.

The single-vineyard barolos, especially, demonstrate how careful selection can lead to first-class results. The *crus* around the winegrowing community of Castiglione Falletto, the headquarters of the house, are among the best-known barolo slopes. Currado and Cordero have taken full advantage of them: the barolos Rocche and Brunate are highly concentrated but elegant wines, the Barbera d'Asti from the neighboring vineyard Scarrone is also extremely successful.

Once he began planting an increasing amount of nebbiolo, known as "the pearl of the Piedmont," Currado decided to use the nebbiolo pomaces for making grappa.

Grappa di Nebbiolo

Distilled in pot stills from thoroughly fermented pomaces from the Vietti winery at the Montanaro distillery in Gallo d'Alba; standard quality at 90 proof, 70 cl.

🍷 *A clear, appetizingly fresh brandy with a very soft aroma of compote, a breath of licorice, and grassy notes; round, complex, and harmonious body that develops a voluptuous warmth on the palate; fiery, almost oily finish.*

Grappa di Nebbiolo da Barolo "Rocche"

From the fully fermented pomaces of the single-vineyard Barolo Rocche, in the winegrowing commune of Castiglione Falletto. Distilled in pot stills immediately after racking in San Marzanotto, at the small Fratelli Rovero estate distillery in a limited quantity of only 400 bottles. Aged for four years in small oak barrels (86 proof, 50 cl).

🍷 *Light gold, very aromatic grappa; floral bouquet with vanilla tones and a harmonious herbal nose. Soft, heavy body with a round, full aroma and an almost flat finish filled with hints of dried fruits. An extremely dry brandy.*

ZARDETTO

ZARDETTO SPUMANTI S.N.C.
VIA MARCORÀ, 15
31020 SCOMICO DI CONEGLIANO, VENETO

An estate founded in 1969 by the enologist Pino Zardetto in the homeland of the fashionable sparkling prosecco. In addition to dry white wines with the DOC Cartizze and Prosecco di Conegliano, trendsetter Zardetto has devoted himself in recent years to the production of sparkling wines from the prosecco grape, using a variant of the Charmat method typical of the Veneto but with longer yeast fermentation. He has thereby considerably improved the quality of prosecco, which is still inexpensive but trying to make a name for itself all over Europe.

Conegliano's castello

LA GRAPPA DI PINO ZARDETTO

*Single-variety grappa from the prosecco grape, distilled in small,
steam-heated pot stills by Sandro Bottega in Pianzano and aged a
short time in oak barrels (84 proof, 75 cl).*

🍷 *An appealing distillate with a slightly exotic aroma reminiscent of violets and other flowers. Round, soft body.*

GRAPPA ZARDETTO CARTIZZE

*Single-variety prosecco grappa from the high
Cartizze in Conegliano, distilled at the Bottega
distillery (100 proof, 75 cl).*

🍷 *A pungent, masculine brandy
with mellow earthy and animal
notes in its aroma, along with
hints of sandalwood and hay. Rich
and round on the palate with a
muscular, long-lasting finish.*

ZENATO

ZENATO
VIA SAN BENEDETTO, 8
37010 PESCHIERA DEL GARDA, VENETO

*T*he vineyards in the favorable climate south of Lake Garda—more precisely between Deszenzano and Peschiera del Garda, in the provinces of Brescia and Verona—are the home of a rare Vino Lugana, a fresh, spritzig white wine with a pale green shimmer made mainly from trebbiano di Lugana.

One of its best producers is the Zenato family, which makes one of the outstanding examples of the vintage on its twenty-hectare (forty-nine-acre) estate Santa Cristina—the single-vineyard Lugana Vigneto Massoni. These quality wine makers also produce strong red wines of the traditional type (Amarone della Valpolicella) as well as wines in the more modern style (Cabernet Sauvignon Santa Cristina), both of which enjoy high repute.

GRAPPA DI LUGANA

A single-variety pomace distillate from the skins of the trebbiano di Lugana, distilled twice in steam-heated copper stills and harmonized in glass flasks (86 proof, 50 cl).

❦ *A grappa like a basket filled with assorted nuts: a soft, creamy aroma of hazelnut, walnut, and Brazil nuts, refreshingly winy on the palate with a consistent development. A definite success.*

ZENI

AZIENDA AGRICOLA ROBERTO ZENI
VIA L. ADIGE
38010 GRUMO DI SAN MICHELE ALL'ADIGE, TRENTINO

A winery founded in 1882 that now belongs to Roberto Zeni. For more than twenty years Zeni has been one of the most innovative wine makers in the Trentino, one who has created wines not only of international stature but also of a wholly unique character. His are modern wines that nevertheless do not disguise their origins.

Along with his brother Andrea, Zeni distills his grappas from his own single-variety pomaces using the classic double-bottomed pot still of the Trentino. He then ages his distillates on the estate until they are fully mature—in his opinion, this takes much longer than the length of time prescribed by law. As a result of his determined search for quality, his grappas are real finds for both novices and more discriminating buyers. In our opinion he is one of the best grappa producers, and we recommend his brandies highly.

GRAPPA TRENTINA DI MOSCATO ROSA (1994)

From pomaces of moscato rosa from the vineyard Rosa di San Michele. Limited to 3,390 bottles (80 proof, 70 cl).

Our sample no. 1,693: A lighthearted, floral grappa with a pure bouquet of roses and pleasantly strong accents on the palate—the perfect translation of the aromatic moscato rosa.

GRAPPA TRENTINA DI CHARDONNAY (1996)

Distilled in a limited edition of 2,990 bottles from chardonnay pomaces from the Zaraosti vineyard (86 proof, 70 cl).

🍷 *Our sample no. 1,613: An enormously aromatic distillate, youthful and fresh with a delicate, winy aroma of bouquet garni and pure yeast, distinctly riper on the palate, with a dry, intense finish. Unquestionably one of the best of the chardonnay grappas.*

GRAPPA TRENTINA DI TEROLDEGO (1988)

From teroldego pomaces from the Pini des Campo Rotaliano; aged for a long time in small wooden barrels (80 proof, 70 cl). Limited to 3,304 bottles.

🍷 *A microcosm of scents: autumnal, fresh, spicy, creamy, earthy, winy. One needs to take time to enjoy fully this highly complex aroma. Elegant body and wonderfully soft, accentuated finish—a magnificent brandy.*

Additional
Grappas

GRAPPA
TRENTINA
SORTI

GRAPPA
TRENTINA
ALAMBICCO

GRAPPA
TRENTINA
DI PINOT
BIANCO

ACQUAVITE
DI ALBICOC-
CHE

Distillers
A *to* Z

Introduction to the Distillers

*G*rappa is now produced in virtually all the wine regions of Italy. But its homeland is northern Italy, at the foot of the Alps, where at one time the leftovers from wine making were all that peasants and day laborers could use to distill the alcohol that helped them get through the winter and forget their woes. In the fall, distillers would move from village to village with portable stills, processing the leftover pomaces of small winegrowers— and not always legally (moonlighting and smuggling were widespread). Compared to the medieval princes, the Hapsburgs who eventually ruled northern Italy imposed only a modest tax on distilled spirits, so itinerant distillers were finally able to settle near their customers and establish many of the distilleries that are still in operation today.

Northern Italy offered a favorable environment for the production of grappa in another respect as well—an advantage that was crucial to the quality of the distillate before the invention of modern distilling techniques. To avoid bitter substances in the wine, the pomaces of the acidic grape varieties grown there were not pressed as firmly as those of the more aromatic grapes of the south. Because the leftovers were not so dry, the distillate was clearer and purer than that made from flowery southern varieties. The cooler climate in the mountain villages also slowed the decomposition of the pomaces, another important factor in the production of quality brandies.

Local culinary traditions have also fostered the production of grappa in the cooler north. The native cuisine of this fertile landscape was once so heavy that after-dinner digestive brandies were virtually a necessity. In the warm south, with its lighter fare, they were less common.

It is no wonder, then, that the large, old, most-respected grappa distilleries are found almost exclusively in the north. But these have by no means rested on their laurels. More and more of them have come to think of themselves as the standard-bearers of a grappa culture, the guardians of quality, and they have established local branches in order to shorten the distance between vineyard and distillery. These specialized distilling operations, though not as closely tied to wine making as the actual wine-growers, have given grappa the stature it enjoys today.

BAROZZI

◦

ERNESTO BAROZZI DISTILLERIA DANTE
VIA ISONZO, 5
38060 LIZZANA DI ROVERETO, TRENTINO

*F*amily tradition dictated that Ernesto Barozzi
should become a farmer in the Lagarina Valley,
in the Dolomites, where he was born. He did stay at
home, but he was first drawn to winegrowing and
ultimately to grappa distilling, his true calling. Around
the small still on his ancestral farm he created a proper
distillery, one in which he produces grappa *cuvées* and
liqueurs in addition to single-variety grappas. Barozzi
was one of the first to recognize the value of attractive
packaging. His handmade bottles of Murano glass or
Venetian crystal are collector's items, many of them
classical and elegant, others more whimsical.

GRAPPA GRASPA

*Barozzi's prestige grappa: distilled in single
batches from a well-calculated blend of pomaces
and aged in oak barrels (80 proof, 10 and 50 cl).*
  *A dull gold, highly individual grappa with an
expressive bouquet more like that of a liqueur:
bittersweet, reminiscent of rum-soaked fruit and
orangeade; floral and chocolate notes develop in
its strong taste.*

Additional Grappas
*Roughly twenty different pomace distillates, in-
cluding flavored grappas.*

BERTAGNOLLI

PREMIATA DISTILLERIA G. BERTAGNOLLI
VIA CONTE CARLO MARTINI, 40/42
38016 MEZZOCORONA, TRENTINO

The Bolzano merchant Edoardo Bertagnolli established this distillery with capital from his Austrian wife, Julia von Kreutzenberg, in 1870; after only two years it was awarded a gold medal for the quality of its products and appointed purveyor to the imperial court in Vienna. Today the operation is run by Beppe and Livia Bertagnolli. All the distilling is done in single batches in double-bottomed pot stills. The pomaces come from the region, and for single-variety grappas the old Trentino varieties are preferred. The old still paid for by Julia von Kreutzenberg is still in use: the L'Alambicco di Giulia de Kreutzenberg line includes single-variety grappas and grape and fruit distillates.

GRAPPA SELEZIONE DI GRAPPINO

From a mixture of very fresh Trentino pomaces (84 proof, 70 cl).

Extract-rich, deep-toned brandy with gentle spicy notes, medium-heavy but rounded body, delicate bitter tones in the long finish.

Additional Grappas
GRAPPINO BARRIQUE *and eight single-variety grappas*

BOCCHINO

◦

Distilleria Canallese C. Bocchino & C. s.p.a.
Via G. Giuliani, 30
14053 Canelli, Piedmont

*T*hat an operation's large size does not necessarily mean lower quality is nowhere more apparent than in the Bocchino family business, founded in 1898 and now run by Carlo Micca-Bocchino. Despite a cellar capacity of 2 million liters (528,000 gallons) and a daily distilling capacity of 100,000 kilograms (220 tons) of pomace, the grappas produced here are top quality—in part because Bocchino processes only pomaces from its own vineyards that are carefully prepared for distilling and deliberately kept moist. The distilling technique is continuously updated. Traditional stills heated with steam are used to give the grappa more character, but modern methods are fully exploited as well. The aging of the blond brandies is accomplished in a tufa cellar in barrels of Slovenian oak—another contributor

From the good old days of grappa distilling . . .

. . . to the present-day boom

to their quality. In addition to producing brand-name grappas in large quantities, Carlo and his sister Antonella are interested in unusual distillates. While Carlo devotes himself to the native vine varieties, which he hopes to rescue from extinction by careful planting, Antonella has been inspired by a best-seller. The Patrick Süskind novel *Perfume* gave her the idea of producing floral distillates—for example, from roses or acacia blossoms. She even has hybrid orchids flown in from Japan, macerating them in alcohol before the perfumed liquid is again distilled. She calls her product line "I Fiori."

GRAPPA GRAN MOSCATO

Distilled immediately after fermentation from muscat pomaces from the Asti region. Aged for three years in barrels of Slovenian oak (80 proof, 70 cl).

Light gold in color; fresh, herb-toned aroma with a breath of tropical fruits; sweet vanilla and strong spicy notes develop on the palate.

GRAPPA SIGILLO NERO

A mixture of Piedmontese DOC areas: barbera, nebbiolo, dolcetto, and freisa, only briefly fermented and quickly distilled. Long aging in barrels of Slovenian oak (80 proof, 70 cl).

Gold in tone, a nose like a harmoniously flavored fruit salad: pears, bananas, also spices and a breath of vanilla; takes on bitter accents on the tongue that introduce the creamy-chocolaty finish in a most delightful way.

Grappa Carlo Bocchino

A blend of muscat from Asti and nebbiolo from Barolo. Aged for twelve years in barrels of Slovenian oak (86 proof, 70 cl).

An amber-colored, noble distillate with a rich but lively aroma of ripe fruit and delicate roast aromas (sherry?), strong flavor development with warm spicy tones and a seemingly endless finish. Lovely!

Additional Grappas

Grappa Novella
Grappa Cantina Privata
Grappa di Nebbiolo da Barolo "Antonella Bocchino"
Bocchino Gran Riserva

BONOLLO

Luigi Bonollo e Figli s.n.c.
Via Mosca 5/7
41043 Formigine di Modena, Emilia-Romagna

A family business founded in the Veneto in the mid-
nineteenth century by Giuseppe Bonollo. His son Luigi
moved it to Formigine in Emilia-Romagna after World War I in
order to exploit the new Lambrusco boom for the production of
an equally successful grappa. Today Bonollo is the largest producer of pomace brandies in the world, producing 45 million
bottles of brandy in its five distilleries. Despite this enormous
output, Bonollo is very popular with wine makers as a commission distiller, for the operation offers its quality-conscious clients
short transport routes—Bonollo has a distillery in Tuscany in addition to those in northern and southern Italy. Thanks to its array
of equipment, the winegrower has the choice, even for the small-

The Bonollo distillery—old tradition with new technology

est quantities of grappa, between distilling in a double-bottomed still or with steam, or even using a combined continuous-discontinuous procedure. Wine makers can also have their brandies aged at Bonollo's. The operation has stainless-steel tanks with a capacity of 65 million liters (17 million gallons) and oak barrels that hold 32 million liters (8.4 million gallons). In 1990, in the traditional distillery in Greve in Chianti, Bonollo developed a beginner's brandy called Consenso, a superb grappa.

GRAPPA CONSENSO RISERVA (1990)

A blend of the Chianti vines sangiovese, canaiolo, and malvasia, distilled twice and aged separately in barrels of acacia, oak, cherry, and ash, then carefully blended after aging into this cuvée *(90 proof, 50 cl).*

🍷 *A breath of cool autumn, with a pleasant nuttiness and grassy citrus notes, quite sweet in taste but round, soft, becoming warmer toward the finish.*

GRAPPA CONSENSO (1991)

A blend of the Chianti vines, mostly canaiolo, distilled twice (90 proof, 50 cl).

🍷 *A reserved, elegant brandy with a fresh spicy nose and a breath of sweetness; winy body with toast aromas developing on the palate.*

BOTTEGA

⊶◇⊷

Distilleria di Sandro Bottega & C. s.n.c.
Via S. Urbano, 18
31010 Pianzano di Godega, Veneto

*S*andro Bottega's distillery in the Conegliano in the Veneto is a stronghold of the designer grappas currently so fashionable. Representing the third generation of the family, Bottega took over the firm in 1983, only seven years after his father had moved it to Pianzano di Godega in the Conegliano region in 1977. He immediately adapted his production to the demands of the market. His first single-variety grappas were made from chardonnay and cabernet. After visiting distilleries in Brazil, the land of sugarcane brandies, he developed a new distilling technique that proved to be ideal for the native prosecco grape.

With its Bottega Club and Alexander Society lines, marketed in bottles of delicate Treviso glass, the house established its reputation among dealers and owners of fine restaurants. The most-modern distilling methods are employed; a combination of continuous and single-batch procedures allows for the production of grappas with precisely the characteristics desired, which are then further refined through aging in wood or glass.

Grappa "Charolotte Bottega"

A single-variety chardonnay grappa in the Bottega Club series (86 proof, 70 cl).

An ingratiating grappa with a dense aroma (spices, pitted fruits), which becomes quite sweet on the palate in spite of its pleasantly strong bitter notes.

Grappa "Alexander"

A blend of chardonnay and prosecco from Conegliano, from the Alexander Society series (80 proof, 70 cl).

A floral-scented brandy, almost too sweet, with a breath of spices and herbs; light to medium heavy in taste, with strong fruity notes.

"Grappolo"—Grappa di Prosecco

A single-variety grappa from the Alexander Society series presented in unusual bottles (86 proof, 35 cl).

A dewy fresh grappa with lovely mineral tones, citrus notes, and a cool, autumnal impression; bitter-accented wininess with a harmonious finish.

Additional Grappas

Twenty grappas, many of them single variety, in handblown designer bottles in the Alexander Society series

Four additional pomace distillates in the Bottega Club series

Grappe Cellini series, a trademark line distilled at Bottega's from a blend of Veneto pomaces (76 proof, 70 cl).

CELLINI BIANCA

A complex and weighty brandy with a ripe fruit; a round, powerful body; and a warm finish.

CELLINI RISERVA

Light blond, with enormous fullness of aroma: herbs, fall leaves, mushrooms, warm spices; medium heavy in taste with a gentle finish. An almost too-polished grappa—one would prefer more rough edges.

BRUNELLO

————◦————

FRATELLI BRUNELLO
VIA G. ROI, 27
36047 MONTE GALDA, VENETO

*E*arnestness and conscientiousness have been Brunello watchwords since the distillery was founded in 1840. Although it has had a checkered history filled with family setbacks, its production of quality distillates has never been compromised. The present director, Maria Brunello, swears by the traditional distilling techniques. Modern presentation in elegant bottles only enhances the appeal of these fine grappas.

GRAPPA LUCENTINO

Aged for four years in small oak barrels, then bottled in 1992 in a limited edition of 600 bottles (86 proof, 50 cl).

Our sample no. 138: A "culinary" grappa, straw blond with green highlights, an appetizing aroma with a fruity sweetness and winy acidity; harmonious, bittersweet taste with a spicy finish.

Additional Grappas

GRAPPA IL ROCCOLO *and* IL CRUVAJO
  *in limited editions and the same packaging as
  the* GRAPPA LUCENTINO
GRAPPA MOSCATO
CABERNET FRANC
STAGIONATA DI MONTEGALDA
GRAPPA DI PURA VINACCIA
GRAPPA ALLE ERBE

CAMEL

DISTILLERIA CAMEL S.P.A.
VIALE TRICESIMO, 95
33100 POVOLETTO DI UDINE, FRIULI

A classic grappa distillery that favors somewhat old-fashioned bottles with colorful 1950s-style labels. No beauties, but the contents are nonetheless a treat for the nose and palate—an experience not to be missed if you get the chance.

GRAPPA VITE D'ORO (1990)

Made from Friuli pinot, tocai, merlot, and Riesling; distilled continuously and aged for three years in oak barrels (80 proof, 70 cl).

A complex grappa with personality, an appetizing aroma of herbs, sorrel, citrus, grasses, and spices; on the palate expressive and spicy, with a touch of sharpness in the finish. Conceivable as an aperitif before heavy foods.

Additional Grappas

GRAPPA VITE D'ORO *of various ages*

GRAPPA CAMEL SELEZIONE VECCHIA 800, *twenty-five years old*

Various older vintage grappas

CAPOVILLA

Vittorio Capovilla & C. s.n.c.
Ca' Dolfin, Via Giardini, 12
36027 Rosà, Veneto

*M*onte Grappa, a foothill of the Maritime Alps, rises a full 1,775 meters (5,822 feet) above a fertile plain between Vicenza and Venice. Despite the many industrial complexes, this is a landscape still dominated by orchards and vineyards, agricultural production, and a peaceful way of life. Precisely the right setting for the gardener's son Vittorio Capovilla, who after restless years as a race car driver, auto mechanic, and wine steward discovered his talent for distilling and settled down. He was attracted by the small village of Rosà, only a few miles from Bassano del Grappa, a stronghold of grappa distilling. In the cellars of the historic Villa Dolfin, dating from 1760, he set up a distilling operation in accordance with his own specifications.

In the beginning, the quality-mad distiller would drive around the neighborhood himself with a truck and ladder, gathering ripe fruit in overgrown fields or hunting down native grape varieties of the Veneto like Isabella, Noah, or Clinto that were growing wild. His neighbors soon figured out what he was up to and gladly made their harvests available to him, even delivering their fresh pomaces after pressing. Carefully mashed and fermented with natural yeasts without any sort of additives, these raw materials are then immediately distilled.

He distills twice in a double-bottomed copper still, the classic Veneto distilling vessel. On average, Capovilla's brandies age for two years before they are cut to drinking strength with pure spring water and bottled. With his brandies being regularly singled out in blind tastings, Capovilla is considered to be a rising star on the Italian distilling scene.

Grappa di Bassano (1993)

*A vintage grappa from a blend of Veneto vines, carefully distilled
in a double-bottomed pot still and harmonized for two years in
glass (82 proof, 70 cl).*

▮ *An ingratiating distillate with a full, round aroma dominated by dark tones and a delicately bitter tone in the long finish.*

Distillato d'Uva Isabella Selvatica

*A grape distillate from the pomaces of the wild Isabella vine, gen-
tly pressed and distilled twice immediately after fermentation
(82 proof, 50 cl).*

▮ *A highly individual grape brandy
with dry aroma of powerful floral
tones, yellow fruits, and nuts over an
ample body—most appetizing and
delightful!*

Additional Grappas

Grappa di Moscato Diallo
Distillato d'Uva
Distillato d'Uva Clinto
Distillato d'Uva Noah

CASTELLO DI BARBARESCO

DISTILLERIA DEL BARBARESCO
LOCALITÀ BRICCO ALBANO
12050 BARBARESCO, PIEDMONT

*T*he Castello di Barbaresco distillery has long been known to grappa lovers. Though it has frequently changed course through the years, it has always stood for quality. Started as a distillery for various "Produttori di Barbaresco," it later became the house distillery for the famous Bruno Giacosa. Now it is run by the top Piedmontese wine maker Angelo Gaja, who distills here his single-vineyard wines and *cuvées* under his own name and also makes grappa from the pomaces from other quality wines. Here you truly sense that the essence of a region is captured in its brandies— the results speak for themselves.

GRAPPA SITO MORESCO

A single-vineyard and single-variety grappa from the pomaces of the noble Piedmontese nebbiolo grape, harvested in the Gaja vineyards of the Sito Moresco in the Barbaresco district; distilled twice in single batches and harmonized in stainless-steel tanks (84 proof, 70 cl).

An extremely elegant, reasonably smooth grappa with a reserved, nut-accented aroma and a consistent development. Increasing strength on the palate before a dry, delicately bitter finish.

CHARISMA

GRAPPA-HAUS
EUGEN-RICHTER-STRASSE 11/34
34134 KASSEL, GERMANY

*C*harisma is the German brand name of the Grappa-Haus firm, specializing in imported grappa and Italian wines. It is produced by the small but highly respected distillery Sannazzaro, in Lombardy. Charisma's distiller, Giovanni Mariani, has been involved in the production of high-alcohol-content spirits for more than forty years, first as cofounder of the bitters producer Brambilla Liquori (Amaro Bram), and since 1976 with his Distillerie Sannazzaro.

Since 1994 his son Antonio has been helping him in the highly professional operation that produces mainly single-variety grappas from pomaces from Lombardy and neighboring Piedmont. In addition to the Charisma line, Sannazzaro has its own exclusive Convento series presented in whimsical and highly original designer bottles.

GRAPPA DI LAMBICCO

A cuvée of Piedmont pomaces distilled twice in single batches and harmonized for more than six months in stainless steel (84 proof, 50 cl).

A highly expressive distillate with a smooth, winy signature and enormous development of strength along with a successful balance between sweetness and spice—highly individual and altogether delightful!

Grappa Stravecchia

A barrel-aged grappa from a blend of Piedmontese pomaces, distilled twice with steam in single batches (84 proof, 50 cl).

🍷 *A light gold brandy with a spice-dominated fruity nose and a warm, soft body. Elegant finish with delicate bitter tones.*

Grappa Barolo Brillante

A single-variety grappa from nebbiolo pomaces from the Barolo district, distilled twice in a copper pot still and aged for several years in small oak casks (84 proof, 50 cl).

🍷 *The virtual prototype of a Barolo grappa; radiant gold in color, a round, complex aroma (flowers, melons, pistachio, marzipan), and a harmonious development clear into the long, appetizing finish. A superb product full of, yes, charisma.*

Additional Grappas

The CHARISMA *line:* GRAPPA BIANCA INVECCHIATA, BARRIQUE, *and* CRI-SOL BRILLANTE

The CONVENTO *line: Single-variety grappas from pinot, prosecco, chardonnay, verduzzo, muscat, and nebbiolo da Barolo*

DA PONTE

——◦►——

Distilleria Andrea Da Ponte
Via Matteotti, 6
31015 Conegliano, Veneto

*O*ne of the oldest distilleries in Italy, now owned by the descendants of the Andrea Da Ponte who founded the firm in 1892. Supported by the technical know-how of his brother Matteo Da Ponte, a developer and manufacturer of distilling machinery, Andrea Da Ponte set out to produce grappas from the pomaces of prosecco grapes, the most important variety in Conegliano, using the vacuum device prescribed by the Da Ponte–Comboni method. In 1968 this Vecchia Grappa di Prosecco was honored with the Bacco d'Oro prize.

VECCHIA GRAPPA DI PROSECCO

A cuvée *of eight prosecco pomace distillates of various vintages aged in small casks of Limousin oak (84 proof, 70 cl).*
Light gold, with a lovely prosecco bouquet: fresh, spritzig, winy, ripe-tasting with fruity chocolate-citrus tones and a slightly tingling finish.

DISTERCOOP

DISTERCOOP S.C.A.R.L.
VIA GRANAROLO, 231
48018 FAENZA, VENETO

The firm La Crude from Barbiano markets Distercoop distillates under the trade name "Note d'Autore"—grappas precisely tailored to current tastes and at a universally tolerable 80 proof in appealing, modern packaging. Typical mass goods? Not at all. Both the blended grappa and the single-variety Müller-Thurgau are perfectly respectable, appealing digestives that are fully able to compete with their nobler competitors.

NOTE D'AUTORE

Pleasantly round, mature, and flowery distillate with a light spice note and a winy, spicy body; long finish with a breath of vanilla (70 cl).

NOTE D'AUTORE MÜLLER-THURGAU

A surprisingly fresh brandy with clean yeast notes and elegant aromas of fruit and summer flowers; fruity, nutty impressions develop on the palate; becomes warmer in the long finish. A highly individual and lovely grappa (50 cl).

DOMENIS

DISTILLERIA EMILIO DOMENIS & FIGLI S.N.C.
VIA DARNAZZANO, 16
33043 CIVIDADE DEL FRIULI, FRIULI

*A*n old family distillery that uses the most up-to-date techniques. It makes both classic grappas from mixed pomaces and single-variety brandies.

ACQUAVITE D'UVA FRAGOLINO

Distilled in single batches (84 proof, 50 cl).

🍷 *A dry, masculine distillate with a mineral-toned aroma of herbs and citrus fruits; ripe fruit and mushroom tones develop on the palate, growing warmer in the finish.*

GRAPPA FRIULANA

Aged four years, two of them in oak casks (86 proof, 70 cl).

🍷 *A pleasantly full-bodied grappa with clear structure, a winy fresh nose of green apples, grass, and white wine grapes; great development of strength in the final stretch.*

A vineyard in Friuli

FRANCESCHINI

---◦►---

DISTILLERIA BRUNO FRANCESCHINI
AZIENDA AGRICOLA COLLE DEGLI OLIVI
VIA VILLA, 12
37010 CAVAION VERONESE, VENETO

*A*n old, established, highly esteemed distillery in the tiny wine village of Cavaion Veronese, between Verona and Bardolino. The gently rolling garden landscape between Soave and Lake Garda is one of the loveliest and most fertile regions of northern Italy: cypresses shade vines tied into tall pergolas, and a spicy scent of flowers hangs in the air—quintessential Italy.

For the distiller Bruno Franceschini, his location between the growing regions for Bardolino Classico and Valpolicella Classico has additional advantages: thanks to the proximity of quality wine producers, his distillery has constant access to high-quality fresh pomaces from which he distills single-variety grappas typical of the region. He uses only moist, fully fermented raw materials.

He distills in two classic copper pot stills, one heated with steam, the other employing the more elaborate water-bath method. According to Franceschini, a distiller requires patience more than anything else. The moist grape skins are heated slowly, at moderate temperatures. The resulting brandy is further distilled until it reaches an alcohol level of 75 percent by volume. It is then harmonized for at least six months in stainless steel or glass and filtered at low temperature after having been diluted to drinking strength.

One of Franceschini's specialties is a grappa made from white passita grapes that have dried on straw mats until February and have to be fermented with extreme care after pressing—yielding a rarity with a character all its own.

Grappa Bianca di Recioto Amarone

From the skins of Amarone della Valpolicella that have been dried before pressing, distilled twice, and allowed to harmonize for a long time (90 proof, 70 cl).

A muscular athlete: a strong aroma of earth and flowers and an intense, pleasantly sweet taste well into the endless finish.

Grappa di Recioto Amarone

A barrel-aged grappa from pomaces of the recioto amarone, the Valpolicella specialty. Distilled twice in copper stills and aged in wood (90 proof, 70 cl).

Deep gold; complex, fresh aroma impressions (grasses, nuts, mint, chocolate); winy-warm body with a certain sharpness in the dry finish. A true maverick.

Additional Grappas

Bardolino Invecchiata
Soave Bianca
Fermentino Bianca
Vinacce di Uva Passita
  Bianca

FRANCOLI

**Fratelli Francoli s.p.a.
Corso Romagnano, 20
28074 Ghemme, Piedmont**

*T*his family operation wasn't established until 1951, but it now exports its grappas all over the world. One of Italy's largest grappa producers, it processes 5,000 tons of pomace a year and turns out 600,000 bottles, yet quality is its chief concern. It does all of its distilling with steam in copper alembics, in a process it developed and patented. Aging of the white brandies is accomplished mainly in stainless-steel tanks, but for roughly eighteen days they are also allowed to rest in *barriques* of Limousin oak. Brandies selected for barrel aging are first harmonized in steel tanks for six months, then transferred to barrels of Slovenian oak with capacities between 225 and 15,000 liters (59 to 3,960 gallons). A final inspection is performed with a gas chromatograph before bottling, to make sure there are no undesired aroma components. The distillery maintains a welcoming visitors center.

Grappa d'Lambic

From 40 percent nebbiolo, 40 percent dolcetto, and 20 percent muscat pomaces (86 proof, 50 cl).

🍸 *A winy fresh distillate with a delicate orange bouquet from the muscat and earthy, oily notes; complex, full-bodied fruit aromas in the taste, which becomes increasingly sweet.*

Grappa I Segreti Moscato

🍷 *Lively, with intense fruit nose (orangeade, grapes, a breath of spice), a medium-heavy body, and enduring strength in the finish. A consistent, very lovely muscat grappa (90 proof, 50 cl).*

Oro di Barolo

From nebbiolo grapes from the barolo slopes of Monforte, Barolo, La Morra, and Grinzane Cavour, fermented in the distillery and aged for more than four years in barrels of oak from the Limousin, Allier, and Cher. A cuvée of distillates of various ages (84 proof, 50 cl).

🍷 *A strong, elegant brandy with lush fruit (plums, peaches) and a breath of bitter almonds; soft, round body with a definite wininess.*

Additional Grappas

Grappa Bianca
Grappa Invecchiata
Grappa Grand Cru
Grappa Riserva,
 ten years old

GIORI

GIORI G.I.L.S.A. S.R.L.
VIA NAZIONALE, 38
38060 VOLANO, TRENTINO

*F*erruccio Gior established his distillery in Rovereto, in the Trentino, forty years ago, devoting himself to large-scale distillation of grappa in the traditional manner. In 1972, after moving to neighboring Volano, he also began making fruit brandies, though grappa continues to be the focus of his worldwide marketing activities.

In addition to classic single-variety grappas from nosiola, teroldego, marzemino, and muscat, he now distills a chardonnay, following the recent trend, and offers three *cuvées* tailored to different tastes. He also offers a prestige line in unusual packaging, grappa liqueurs, and the two vintage grappas Mozart and Amadeus, introduced in the Mozart year 1991—a bow to the musical genius who spent some time in the Trentino. All the distilling is accomplished in single batches in double-bottomed pot stills.

GRAPPA DI MOSCATO

A single-variety muscat grappa from the standard line
Tradizione del Trentino (80 proof, 70 cl).

A very lovely, clearly structured grappa with a winy fruit aroma, surprisingly powerful taste, and an explosive development of orange and chocolate aromas in the medium-long finish.

GRAPPA DI MOSCATO

From the premium line Selezione Elite, a single-variety muscat grappa in a limited edition of 1,740 liters (86 proof, 50 cl).

🍷 *A well-aged, concentrated brandy with an abundant muscat aroma: light spicy tones, juicy blood oranges, herbs; muscular and masculine in taste, with definite orange notes in the long, intense finish.*

Additional Grappas

SELEZIONE ELITE: *Single-variety grappas from teroldego, nosiola, marzemino, and chardonnay in handblown glass vials*

GRAPPA TRENTINA *series: The cuvées Novella, Preziosa, and Gentile*

TRADIZIONE DEL TRENTINO *series: Chardonnay, teroldego, marzemino, and nosiola*

LINEA PRESTIGIO *series: Handmade glass ampoules with a handblown vine inside and filled with classic Trentino grappas*

INGA

─◦─

Distillerie Inga & C. s.r.l.
Via Garibaldi, 10
15069 Serravalle Scrivia, Piedmont

*O*ne of the oldest distilleries in the Piedmont, established in 1832—just at the time when Turin and Milan were gaining international reputations as centers of the spirits trade, when Campari and Cinzano were invented, and Martini and Rossi became partners. The original Gambarotta firm was renamed Inga in 1938, and since 1979 its various grappa lines have been marketed under this name. In good years up to 25,000 tons of pomace and grapes are processed in the distillery. Its raw materials come from the DOC regions of Alba, Barolo, Ovada, Gavi, Vignale Monferrato, and Asti in the Piedmont and neighboring Oltrepò Pavese in Lombardy. Short delivery routes and precise scheduling ensure that the pomaces are still fresh on arrival and are immediately distilled in small copper alembics gently heated with steam. In addition to single-variety grappas and grappa *cuvées* from the Gavi region or

the Piedmont, Inga also produces brandy, Amaro, Sambuca, and various liqueurs. For fanciers of ancient and modern glass, it has introduced two special bottlings: the Grappa di Vitigno Brachetto in a reproduction of the historic Clessydra bottle from France, the original of which is owned by the Inga family, and the Grappa di Nebbiolo da Barolo in a handblown crystal bottle designed and produced by the master craftsman Carlo Moretti from Murano.

GRAPPA DI PINOT-CHARDONNAY

A lovely, unusual brandy that reveals all four basic tastes in its aroma: sweet, bitter, sour, salt. Bittersweet on the palate with chocolaty spice notes and a piquant finish (84 proof, 50 cl).

GRAPPA DI GAVI DI GAVI

A delicate grappa with a floral bouquet, hints of mushrooms, nuts, and fruit; the light body seems winy and spicy at first, but becomes sweeter in the finish (84 proof, 50 cl).

GRAPPA DI NEBBIOLO DA BAROLO

An aroma-intensive distillate with a rich scent of oranges, flowers (violets?), citrus notes, and grapes; amazingly spicy in taste with plenty of backbone and a slight peppery finish. An appetizing grappa that would go wonderfully with a fall menu (84 proof, 50 cl).

Additional Grappas

Single-variety grappas from barolo, dolcetto, gavi, grignolino, muscat, and pinot nero, and luxury grappas in handblown bottles.

Red-grape pomaces yield expressive grappas

JULIA

---◦▸---

Stock s.p.a.
Via Lionello Stock, 2
34135 Trieste, Friuli

*I*n 1884, at eighteen, Lionello Stock left Dalmatia for Trieste and immediately saw his chance. Why not distill the wines of the region, then mostly being sold to France for the production of cognac, and sell his own "cognac" in the Austrian empire? With his partner Carlo Camis, he set up a small steam distillery in Trieste's Barcola quarter—the beginnings of the present-day multinational Stock firm. To its "Cognac Medicinal," renamed "Brandy Stock 84" in 1955 in response to French objections to its use of the name "cognac," the firm later added the grappa brand Julia, made of pomaces from Dalmatia, Istria, and the Veneto. Today it is distilled from Italian pomaces exclusively and presented in three grades. The single-variety Goccia line is a recent addition. All together, Stock produces 16 million bottles of alcoholic beverages a year, exporting to 125 countries.

Julia Superiore

(76 proof, 50 cl)
Nutty, ripe fruit, spice notes, and a hint of bitterness in the nose; sweetish and soft on the palate, with a lasting sweet, almost liqueurlike finish.

Celsa-Grappa di Pinot-Cabernet

(88 proof, 70 cl)
Spritzig and fresh at the start, then developing depth and a fruity warmth with strong spice notes. An appealing grappa with a refreshing finish.

GOCCIA DI PROSECCO

(90 proof, 70 cl)

Straightforward but delicate distillate with a spritzig-fresh prosecco nose that gains increasing warmth into the strong and piquant finish.

Additional Grappas

GRAPPA JULIA BIANCA
GOCCIA DI PINOT CHARDONNAY
GOCCIA DI VERDUZZO

MANGILLI

MANGILLI S.P.A.
VIA TRE AVIERI, 12
33030 FLUMIGNANO DI TALMASSONS, FRIULI

*U*ntil only a few years ago, this distillery in a village south of Udine was owned by the marchesi Mangilli. More than a hundred years ago, in 1894, the head of the family, Fabio Mangilli, took up grappa distilling as a hobby, presenting his products to friends and acquaintances. Only after World War II did the family begin commercial production of fine brandies, relying on the old, traditional pot stills despite extensive plant modernization. Marchese Babio Mangilla took on Francesco Perissinotto as a partner in 1977, so as to be able to devote himself more intensively to his horsemanship, which had already won the nobleman an Olympic medal. Perissinotto, whose grandfather Silvio Barbieri had invented the liqueur Apero, was for a long time the director of the Distilleria Barbieri. In his new function he enlarged Mangilli, adding a continuous distilling apparatus and a grape-pressing facility, and in 1991 he took over the firm completely. Since 1994, in addition to the three standard grappas Bianca, Riserva, and Collezione, he has been producing a selection of grape brandies.

BIANCA

(90 proof, 70 cl)
A deep bouquet with fruity spice notes that gain in sharpness on the palate up into the piquant, peppery finish—a round, mellow, Indian summer grappa.

RISERVA

(90 proof, 70 cl)

Sophisticated. A rich gold; expressive aroma of fruit (especially oranges and plums), autumnal associations, and ripe secondary aromas; piquant and accentuated on the palate, with a deep sweetness that adds a delicate bitterness at the finish.

COLLEZIONE

(90 proof, 50 cl)

Lighter gold; fruity impression with plums and acacia that introduces a spicy undertone; youthful, fiery appeal with a slightly peppery finish.

MAROLO

DISTILLERIA S. TERESA DEI FRATELLI MAROLO
VIA CASE SPARSE, 35
12067 MUSSOTTO D'ALBA, PIEDMONT

A newcomer among distilleries. Established by the Marolo brothers only in 1977, the operation has been in part responsible for the triumph of fine grappas and their present-day cachet. It all began with the pomaces of wine-making friends that the brothers distilled on consignment. But then they decided to elevate their grappa to the level that the wines of their native Piedmont had long since achieved. Contracts were concluded with quality-conscious winegrowers whose vineyards were among the best in the region. Quite early, for example, they established relations with the Soldati family from the vineyard La Scolca in Cavi, inventors of the highly successful wine type Gavi di Gavi, now recognized with its own DOC. Also Marchese Paolo Cordero di Montezemolo, famed as the initiator of the "new wave" in Barolo, consigned the pomaces from his Monfalletto estate to the Marolo brothers—a tradition that continues to this day.

Each pomace was distilled separately and the distillate distinguished by vine variety and place of origin, as was customary in the Langhe, or southern Piedmont. A comprehensive program with small editions of highly individual and varied grappas was the result. The brothers commissioned the farmer, artist, and woodcarver Gianni Gallo to design their labels, so that each variety has its own distinctive appearance. They also selected imaginative bottles of elegantly thin crystal. Ugo Marolo has withdrawn from the business, and his brother Paolo, previously responsible only for the technical side and a teacher at the wine-making school in Alba, is now solely in charge of the operation. He continues to hold to tradition, doing all of his distilling in single batches in double-bottomed stills. His total output is a mere 35,000 bottles a year.

Grappa di Arneis

Distilled from skins of the rare arneis grape from the Roero district, on the left bank of the Tanaro. Limited edition of roughly 700 liters (185 gallons) (100 proof, 50 and 70 cl).
A typical white wine grappa: fresh as a cool breeze, grassy green, with intense wininess and a spicy body; distinctly appetizing.

Grappa Barbaresco Montestefano

A barbaresco grappa from the Montestefano slopes (84 proof, 50 cl).
Perfectly balanced between sweetness and bitterness, gentle in its aroma and warm, with hints of mushrooms and bitter almonds; on the palate the bitter tones increase and the finish is chocolaty sweet.

Grappa di Gavi dei Gavi "La Scolca" (1988)

From pomaces of white cortese from the La Scolca estate. In 1988 only 1,600 liters (422 gallons) of this grappa were produced (94 proof, 50 and 70 cl).

An especially imposing grappa, luscious and round, with the aromas of a fruit basket full of mangos, papayas, apricots, peaches; winy on the palate, with spicy notes developing in the finish.

Additional Grappas

Single-variety grappas: Dolcetto, nebbiolo, pigato, vermentino, muscat, freisa, pelaverga, and bracchetto

Grappa di Barolo: *A nebbiolo grappa aged for four years in acacia wood barrels*

Grappa Dedicata al Padre: *A grappa* cuvée *of bracchetto, bonarda, grignolino, and nebbiolo*

Grappa dei Poderi Monfalletto dei Marchesi Cordero di Montezemolo

MAROLO, UGO

Grapperia S. Anna di Ugo Marolo s.r.l.
Strada Borra
12051 S. Vittorio d'Alba, Piedmont

*U*go Marolo first presented his new grappa at the wine fair VinItaly in Verona in 1993. Having left the S. Teresa distillery only a short time before (see previous listing), Marolo could be proud of his new Grapperia S. Anna, and grappa lovers are grateful to him.

Grappa di Nebbiolo da Barbaresco

At a full 86 proof, a stimulating, piquant brandy. With its rich, harmonious fruit and spicy herbal notes—which intensify on the palate into unbridled strength with a strong touch of bitterness in the long, orange-toned finish—it manages to please more than just fans of high-percentage distillates.

Additional Grappas
Grappa di Nebbiolo da Barolo
Grappa di Chardonnay
Grappa di Dolcetto
Grappa Gocce di Langa Moscato
Grappa di Moscato
Grappa di Nebbiolo

MASCHIO

—◦▸—

Bonaventura Maschio
Via Vizza, 2
31018 Gaiarine, Veneto

*A*distillery established by Bonaventura Maschio in 1919. The founder was able to use the stills and a knowledge of distilling inherited from his father. Still owned by the family, the operation has become a leader in the production of *distillati d'uve,* for which it hopes to find increasing numbers of customers. A new copper distilling apparatus was designed specifically for the production of grape brandies, one that would preserve a distinctly grapy character and fruity softness. The house is equally concerned with achieving a similar softness in its grappas. After distillation—using a combination copper still and copper column—the Grappa Rabosa, called the "Velvet Grappa" (Grappa di Velluto), is aged for six months in *barriques* before maturing for several years in 2,000-liter (528-gallon) casks.

Grappa Rabosa

From pomaces of the Veneto's rare rabosa grape, aged for several years in oak (84 proof, 70 cl).

Single-batch distilling

▮ *A highly complex, enchanting grappa that is almost white blond in color: light fullness of aromas (grass, citrus, spices, ripe fruits) against a winy, grapy*

background; harmonious, full taste with well-integrated secondary aromas; long, elegant finish with a trace of pepper.

PRIME UVE: DISTILLATO D'UVE PROSECCO E RIESLING

Produced by the modified vacuum technique developed for grape distillates, from healthy grapes from the Conegliano growing region fermented for ten days in the distillery (80 proof, 70 cl).

🍷 *A spicy distillate with a buttery Riesling nose, overtones of nuts, grass, almonds, and laurel, winy fresh on the palate, with a strong, elegant finish.*

PRIME UVE: DISTILLATO D'UVA PROSECCO

From whole prosecco di Conegliano grapes (84 proof, 50 cl).

🍷 *A delicately tingling brandy with winy aromas, rather strong on the palate, with a pleasant bitter tone and a long, dry finish.*

MASCHIO, BENIAMINO

Dott. Beniamino Maschio
Via San Michele, 70
31020 San Michele di San Pietro di Feletto, Veneto

*O*ne of the best-known grappa distilleries in Italy. At the beginning of this century, the distiller Giuseppe Maschio came to the Veneto from Transylvania, and as a traveling distiller moved from place to place during the grape harvest. In 1921 he settled with his son Antonio in the small village of Gaiarine, not far from Conegliano. Success was not long in coming. By 1935 Antonio could undertake the move to a larger distillery in the village of San Michele, near San Pietro di Feletto, where the operation is situated to this day.

Antonio's son, Beniamino Maschio, has now taken over the distillery, assisted by his wife, Theresa, and his son Alessandro. His quality criteria are the same as those that made Giuseppe successful. Regional pomaces, only gently pressed and fresh, are distilled as soon as possible after fermentation is complete. Traditional copper distilling vessels heated with steam at low temperatures preserve the fullness of aroma of the grape must and the individual characteristics of each batch. Numerous successes at grappa tastings and competitions attest that the Maschio concept works.

GRAPPA DI PROSECCO

*A single-variety pomace distillate from prosecco skins from the
Conegliano growing region, distilled twice at low temperatures
(84 proof, 70 cl).*

🍷 *A refreshing distillate typical of this variety, with delicate,
highly elegant mineral notes and a floral grapiness, powerful
and spicy into the long finish.*

GRAPPA BRENTÈ

*A pomace cuvée of burgundy varieties and prosecco, distilled
twice and aged for five years in oak barrels (84 proof, 70 cl).*

🍷 *A full-bodied, mature brandy
with great charm: winy,
warm, luxurious, with an appealing harmony between sweetness, wood notes, and delicate
spice; a dry finish.*

Additional Grappas

GRAPPA DI CHARDONNAY
GRAPPA DI MOSCATO
GRAPPA DI RECIOTO
  AMARONE
GRAPPA DI PINOT
GRAPPA DELLA
  FRASCA
GRAPPA DI CHARDON-
  NAY SAN MICHELE
GRAPPA DI CARTIZZE

MAZZETTI D'ALTAVILLA

MAZZETTI D'ALTAVILLA S.R.L.
VIALA UNITÀ D'ITALIA, 2
15041 ALTAVILLA MONFERRATO, PIEDMONT

A family distillery established by Filippo Mazzetti in his hometown of Altavilla in 1846 and now run by the fourth generation. From a simple plant capable only of distilling fresh grappas on contract from wine makers, the operation has grown with the expansion of its aging cellars and new equipment into one of the largest producers, known not only for its classic blended grappas but also for single-variety distillates from the Piedmont and Liguria.

Felice Mazzetti, who died in 1981, was interested in all kinds of alcoholic products and expanded the firm's offerings. A technical improvement he developed in the 1930s made it possible for the first time to market fruits in alcohol, for which Mazzetti has become synonymous in Italy. The inventive distiller was also fascinated by the transformation of alcoholic beverages into vinegar. The balsamic vinegars he eventually developed were approved by the state authority, the Consorzii dell'Aceto Balsamico, and are prized by Italian gourmets. Also popular are the Mazzetti grappas flavored with herbs and fruits.

Part of the firm's success is likely owing to its emphasis on unusual and up-to-date packaging. Its distilling and aging methods are nevertheless traditional. All the distilling is done in single batches in small steam-heated copper stills. Its grappas are aged in oak and, following time-honored custom, barrels of various other woods as well. The aged brandies are then blended into *cuvées*.

Grappa di Pigato

Distilled from pomaces of the rare pigato grape of northern Liguria (86 proof, 70 cl).

An elegant brandy with bitter fruity notes like pineapple, a more winy fruit on the palate that develops into a bittersweet finish with delicate roast aromas.

Grappa di Nebbiolo da Barolo

From pomaces of the nebbiolo of the Barolo DOC, aged in barrels made of various woods (86 proof, 70 cl).

Light gold with green highlights; a fruity fresh aroma with dense herbal notes, winy on the palate with delicate bitter tones—a mature grappa, appealing for its harmony.

MAZZETTI

Pietro Mazzetti
Via Casale, 4
14030 Montemagno, Piedmont

A distillery established in 1846 that is strongly rooted in tradition, distilling in double-bottomed pot stills. Its insistence on continuity is also apparent in its modern but timeless packaging. Its single concession to present-day trends is its production of single-variety grappas from ruché, Brachetto d'Acqui, Barbera d'Asti, Dolcetto d'Asti, and Moscato d'Asti.

Grappa di Moscato

(86 proof, 50 cl)
❙ *A very complex brandy with a rich but fresh fruit aroma, a trace of plums, nuts, and caraway; pleasantly winy and fresh on the palate, with a delicate, bittersweet finish.*

Grappa di Ruché

(86 proof, 50 cl)
❙ *A warm, fruity grappa with delicate spice notes and overtones of late summer ripeness and fullness; well rounded on the palate, with chocolate and spices in the finish.*

NARDINI

BORTOLO NARDINI S.P.A.
PONTE VECCHIO, 2
36061 BASSANO DEL GRAPPA, VENETO

*O*ne of the oldest distilleries in the Veneto. The founder of the firm, the distiller Bortolo Nardini, moved to Bassano from the Trentino in 1779. The history of the town's bridge, first mentioned in 1209 and whose fate is still recalled in one of Italy's most famous songs, induced him to purchase the Osteria del Ponte, which is still the headquarters of the operation and owned by the family. Distilling is accomplished in the Trentino manner in double-bottomed copper stills. The *grapperia* set up by Bortolo Nardini is still lovingly kept up as a shop and museum.

AQUAVITE DI VINACCIA RISERVA

Distilled twice from pinot, tocai, and cabernet pomaces from the Veneto's Piave region and aged in oak barrels (100 proof, 100 cl).

A classic soul warmer: gold, with an appetizing aroma of raisins, stewed plums, and nuts, which takes on a spicy palate toward the finish. From beginning to end a harmonious brandy with consistent development.

NONINO

Distillerie Nonino
Via Aquileia, 104
33050 Percoto, Friuli

*A*ccording to general consensus, Nonino is one of the finest and most important distilleries in Italy. But above all, Nonino is credited with having been a dynamic trendsetter in the development of grappa into a luxury product.

After years of traveling around with his portable still, Orazio Nonino established a permanent operation in Ronchi di Pavia in 1887. That first modest plant attained a regional reputation under his son Vigi and grandson Antonio. In 1929 the distillery was moved to its present location in Percoto, near Udine. The current head of the firm, Benito Nonino, is a great-grandson of the founder. He and his wife, Giannola, have enlarged the plant considerably but have not changed the classic production methods to meet increasing business. As always, Nonino grappas are distilled in single batches in copper stills.

Part of the Nonino tradition has been keeping technically up-to-date. Many of the innovations in the industry over the last thirty years have come from this inventive firm. It was the first to distill the pomaces of different vineyards separately, the first to present vintage grappas (1967) with an indication of the size of the pomace and the number of bottles produced from it. In 1973 it introduced the first modern single-variety grappa, its now legendary Picolit, a distillate of pomaces from the rarest and most delicate grape from Friuli.

Interest in the wine-growing culture of its region also led to Nonino's concentration in the early 1970s on the native vines ribolla gialla, scoppettino, pignolo, and tacelenghe—all threatened with extinction owing to European Commission regulations pushing for uniformity. In 1974 the Noninos funded the Risit d'Aur (golden sprig) prize for research on rescuing regional agricultural traditions, and their efforts were rewarded in 1978 when the old Friulian vine varieties were once again accepted by wine-growing authorities. In 1983 the authorities even recommended planting them. The pomace distillates from these vines, along with picolit, now form the core of the single-variety Grappe di Monovitigno.

In the early 1980s the Noninos again set new standards with the notion of distilling not only more or less moist pomaces but also fermented whole, juicy grapes, aiming for a grappa variant with even more exquisite fruit aroma and a purer, gentler taste. The new product was given official approval on November 27, 1984, and the first "Ùe" (Friulian for grape) was distilled, using picolit grapes. The .75-liter bottles designed for the first Ùe by the Italian architect and designer Franco Vattolo and handmade in Murano in a limited edition of 656 have long since become collectors' items. Ùe acquavite from single-variety grapes are now distilled in six varieties: yellow moscato, fragola, verduzzo, cabernet franc, gewürztraminer, and Müller-Thurgau. There is also the *cuvée* Ùe-Uva from grapes from Friuli and Trentino.

VUISINÂR (1993)

A grappa from select red pomaces from the Grave and Colli Friulani, aged up to three years in small casks made of wild cherry (vuisinâr) *(86 proof, 70 cl).*

♟ *Light gold; spicy aroma with deli-cate wood tones, very clear and pure but complex nose; soft and warm, delightful in both taste and finish.*

Ribolla (1992)

A single-variety grappa, exclusively from pomaces from yellow ribolla grapes from the Colli Friulani, aged from six months to a year in glass or stainless steel (90 proof, 50 cl).

🍷 *White, clear; heavy, sweetish nose with an abundance of autumnal aromas (wild mushrooms, hay); round, distinct, fullbodied taste with hints of pitted fruits; warm, intense finish.*

Ùe Decennale

Part of the first official grape brandy distilled from picolit grapes in 1984, bottled after aging for ten years (86 proof, 70 cl).

🍷 *An enchanting prima donna of grape brandies: an intense but harmonious aroma of grapes with delicate spice from the long aging; full-bodied taste on the palate well into the long finish.*

PAGURA

Domenico Pagura di Liudo Pagura
Via Favetti, 25
33080 Castions di Zoppola, Friuli

*O*ld, established, family-owned distillery that ignores fashion and relies on traditional craftsmanship. Needless to say, it distills in single batches with steam and specializes in such native Friuli grape varieties as muscat, fragola, verduzzo, and refosco. It refrains from adding aroma substances, even though they are permitted. The water for the steam comes from the distillery's own well.

Grappa di Refosco

From pomaces of the red-stemmed refosco, the traditional red grape variety of the Friuli. Limited edition of 13,000 bottles (100 proof, 70 cl).

🍷 *Our sample no. 11,296: a well-balanced grappa with a distinctly nutty accent—soft, creamy, warm, but full of life; becomes more intense in taste, with a winy freshness.*

Additional Grappas

Grappa Invecchiata, *aged for three years in wood barrels*
Grappa di Cabernet
Grappa di Fragola
Grappa di Pinot Grigio
Grappa di Verduzzo
Grappa di Moscato

PIAVE

LANDY FRÈRES S.P.A.
VIA B. BUOZZI, 1
40067 RASTIGNANO, VENETO

A Veneto distillery on the bank of the Piave, established in 1870. In 1987 it was acquired by Seagram Italia. Despite its large production capacity, it strives for quality and adheres to traditional distilling methods enhanced by the most modern techniques. With obvious success: grappas marketed under the Piave name are among the most popular brands in Germany. Like blended whiskey, they are distilled in two parts: one part continuously, the other in single batches with steam, in the manner of the Charentais.

In addition to Grappa Bianca and Grappa Riserva, the house produces two aromatics: a classic Grappa Ruta, perfumed with extracts of rue, and a popular plum grappa based on Grappa Bianca, with aromas and extracts of Veneto plums. Three grape brandies from Müller-Thurgau, Riesling, and sauvignon plus a Sambuca round out the distillery's program.

GRAPPA PIAVE CUORE DI CONEGLIANO VENETO

From pomaces of 70 percent white grapes (verduzzo, Riesling, tocai, and pinot) and 30 percent red (cabernet, rabosa, and merlot), aged at least eight months in oak barrels (80 proof, 70 cl).

An appealingly tart grappa with winy spice and herb notes, sweet orange tones on the palate, and a warm finish. Not exceptionally complex but altogether pleasant.

Grappa Piave Riserva

Based on the Cuore distillate, but aged at least two years in oak barrels (84 proof, 70 cl).

🍷 *The Riserva variant is pale gold, with complex spice aromas, a more striking flavor of herbs and orange, and good development.*

Additional Distillates

Gemma d'Uva series:

Acquavite d'Uva Müller-Thurgau, *a brandy distilled from Trentino grapes*

Acquavite d'Uva Riesling, *brandy from Riesling grapes from the Veneto*

Acquavite d'Uva Sauvignon, *from whole sauvignon grapes from the Veneto growing region*

PILZER

—◄◦►—

DISTILLERIA PILZER S.N.C. DI TABARELLI RITA & C.
VIA PERLAIA, 17
38030 FAVER, TRENTINO

A small family distillery established by Vincenzo Pilzer in 1956 and for some years now operated by his son Bruno. This highly knowledgeable graduate of the San Michele school of wine making and distilling, where he now teaches as well, was able to profit from the practical experience of his father and the professional knowledge of his uncle, the enologist Ivano Pilzer. Bruno Pilzer managed to break through into the front rank of grappa distillers in 1985 with his first single-variety grappas, for which he wisely chose the aromatic Müller-Thurgau and native schiava and nosiola grapes—aromatic varieties that make distillates full of character. In 1989 he added a second still to satisfy the increased demand for Pilzer brandies; both are double-bottomed with water between the walls. Pilzer secures moist pomaces from the winegrowing societies of his native village and neighboring

Bruno and Vincenzo Pilzer

Lavis, also from the Cembra Valley. His traminer pomaces come from the Alto Adige. His annual grappa production amounts to twenty-five thousand 50 cl bottles and four thousand 70 cl bottles.

Grappa di Schiava (1989)

In a limited edition of 2,580 bottles (90 proof, 50 cl) from autumn 1989 from schiava from the Cembra Valley.

Our sample no. 626: The reserved fresh bouquet is reminiscent of a nut basket in fresh grass, with a hint of lemons; in taste gaining volume, with mineral-spritzig notes and warm, clean finish.

Grappa di Traminer

Distilled from traminer pomaces from the Alto Adige, fermented in the distillery (90 proof, 50 cl).

A tart brandy with a green, herb-toned aroma, piquant and fresh, with a breath of iodine and orange; deeper and riper on the palate with strong, dark flavors and a very dry finish.

Additional Grappas

Grappa di Chardonnay
Grappa di Nosiola
Grappa di Pinot Nero
Grappa di Müller-Thurgau

POLI

Distilleria Poli in Schiavon
Località Schiavon
36060 Vicenza, Veneto

*A*s a grappa distiller, Jacopo Poli enjoys the very highest of reputations, and not only in Italy. International gastronomy could not manage without his superb brandies in their elegant crystal bottles.

This was not always the case. Founded by grandfather Giobatta Poli in 1898, the operation was known for good everyday grappas, at best, until the early 1980s. The Polis had simply ignored the trend toward more refined distillates until Jacopo and his siblings Giampaolo, Andrea, and Barbara radically turned the rudder. Now, instead of coarse brandies they set out to produce grappas of the highest quality and with a distinct softness, processing only fresh pomaces and distilling for only six weeks a year, during the grape harvest.

Success has shown that it was the right decision. Their copper distilling apparatus, constructed by their father Tony and continually updated, functions discontinuously with steam, under strict temperature control.

Even the Polis' standard quality, Sarpa di Poli, is in fact a top-quality distillate, using pomaces of 40 percent cabernet and 60 percent merlot, the vines of which have enjoyed optimal conditions in the dry alluvial soil of the Marostica and Breganze hills. They are fermented with the must and delivered immediately after pressing—an essential factor in making a high-class brandy.

The Polis have gone one step further. For several years they have been making not only single-variety grappas, called Amorosa, but also grape distillates (Chiara) and fruit brandies, as well as the brandy L'Arzente.

CHIARA DI UVA FRAGOLA

Grape brandy distilled from the rare "strawberry grape" fragola (86 proof, 50 cl).

🍷 *A highly individual distillate with a rich aroma of strawberries and other berries, round and fresh on the palate, with a delicate acid and peppery bitterness—highly successful.*

AMOROSA DI VESPAIOLO (1992)

Half-fermented pomaces of the native Veneto vespaiolo grape from the hills of Breganze, in a limited edition of 1,620 liters (428 gallons) (86 proof, 10 and 50 cl).

🍷 *Our sample no. 1,459: A truly noble brandy with an intense summery fruit bouquet—gooseberries, apricots, raspberries, peaches; winy in taste, with strong accents of bitter chocolate.*

Additional Grappas

GRAPPE AMOROSA, *from the varieties cabernet, merlot, pinot, and torcolato*

DISTILLATO D'UVA CHIARA, *from the varieties muscat and tocai rosso*

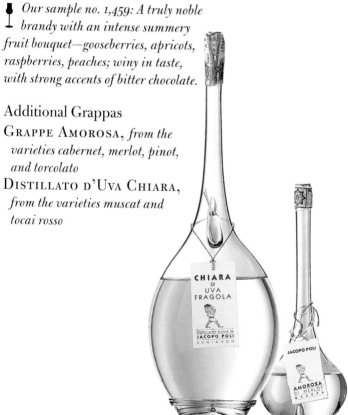

RAMAZZOTTI

DISTILLERIA FRATELLI RAMAZZOTTI S.P.A.
VIA AUSANO RAMAZZOTTI, 21/A
20020 LAINATE, LOMBARDY

*A*usano Ramazzotti, a wine and spirit dealer by trade, was a perfectionist. Dissatisfied with the quality of his merchandise, the Milan native began experimenting, and in 1815 he produced a recipe that would make his name immortal: Ramazzotti. An Amaro made from more than thirty-three different herbs, it is still produced today just outside Milan, exported to over fifty countries, and considered an Amaro classic. Fior di Vite, the grappa of the house, was introduced in 1931 and was received with similar enthusiasm, assuring it a place in the later grappa boom, in which individuality seems to count for more than simple brand recognition. The Fior di Vite offers both: a fine, appealing product in an unusual package—the bottle is sheathed in printed sackcloth.

FIOR DI VITE

Brandy from Piedmont pomaces, mostly muscat grapes. Aged in barrels of Slovenian oak (80 proof, 70 cl).

❦ *A blond distillate with a warm aroma of honey overlaid with fresh citrus notes, extract-rich and warm on the palate, with considerable bitterness: deep, tart, full. Somewhat inharmonious, but pleasant.*

REIMANDI

DISTILLERIA REIMANDI DI CANTINE CA' BIANCA
REGIONE SPAGNA, 50
15010 ALICE BEL COLLE, PIEDMONT

*T*his distillery, originally established in Acqui in 1861, was one of the best in Italy and had been awarded the honorary title "Premiata Distilleria." A few years ago, the quality-conscious wine maker Aureliano Galeazzano acquired the rights to the brand name and moved the operation to Alice Bel Colle. He loves the old winegrowing tradition of the Piedmont. The son of a wine maker, he had already expanded the ancestral estate Ca' Bianca with the addition of eight others in the best locations in the Piedmont. In a major restructuring he determined which of his sites were best for the native vine varieties of his homeland. For the machinery of the old distillery he erected a separate building in which he distills the pomaces from his estates.

GRAPPA MOSCATO

A grappa from the unfermented pomaces of the Piedmontese muscat grape, aged for a very long time in oak barrels and bottled on November 5, 1990, in a limited edition of 737 bottles (86 proof, 50 cl).

Our sample no. 476: Perfection for lovers of very old brandies. A rich gold, a ferny, sherry nose with hints of dried plums and apples; ripe fruit notes on the palate and well-integrated secondary aromas.

RONER

Distilleria Roner s.r.l.
Via Josef von Zallinger, 30
39040 Tramin/Termeno, Alto Adige

A distillery established by Gottfried Roner right after World War II and now owned by his widow, Luisa, and their children. Originally equipped with only a single still, the operation has grown into a concern in which up to 20,000 kilos (22 tons) of pomace are distilled daily—in addition to 45,000 kilos (50 tons) of fruit mash. Roner is the market leader in fruit brandies in Italy. The Roners are also leaders in the search for quality. Their grappa assortment is broad: in addition to the traditional grappas Bianca and Gold from mixed pomaces of local provenance, they produce single-variety grappas from gewürztraminer, Müller-Thurgau, vernaccia, pinot noir, cabernet, and sauvignon pomaces that have not been pressed. The must runs off solely from the weight of the grapes, and as a result the pomaces contain a great deal of moisture. Because of the scarcity of the raw material, the grape brandies Fragolina and Moskatella, from fragola and muscat, are produced in only limited quantities.

Andreas, Margreth, Luisa, Günther, and Franz Roner

GRAPPA SAUVIGNON

(86 proof, 50 cl)

A fresh, clean grappa with a concentrated aroma of grass, citrus fruits, and moist earth; respectable development of strength and a gentle, warm finish.

GRAPPA GEWÜRZTRAMINER

(86 proof, 70 cl)

An aroma-intensive brandy typical of this variety, with floral notes: roses, carnations, summer meadows. Full-bodied and rounded, with developing orange and grapy tones and a profound, slightly nutty finish.

GRAPPA CABERNET

(86 proof, 70 cl)

A consistently structured distillate with a fresh, bright nose: red currants, gooseberries, pistachios, nuts; medium-heavy body with a reserved development and refreshing finish—enchanting.

Additional Grappas

GRAPPA BIANCA
GRAPPA GOLD
GRAPPA RONER RARITAS
GRAPPA PINOT NOIR
GRAPPA VERNATSCH
GRAPPA MÜLLER-
  THURGAU

ROVERO

<hr>

FRATELLI ROVERO DI FRANCO ROVERO & C.
FRAZIONE SAN MARZANOTTO, 216
14050 ASTI, PIEDMONT

A small distillery—with only two single-batch, double-bottomed pot stills—run by Franco and Claudio Rovero on the wine estate Cascina Il Milin. Grappa distilling is a family tradition, ever since the Roveros' great-grandfather moved from vineyard to vineyard distilling pomaces with his portable still in the harvest season from October to January.

His son became a distiller as well, but left to seek his fortune in America. After his distillery in the New World failed, he returned to his hometown. There he laid the foundations of the family estate now owned by the four Rovero siblings, who have built up the distilling of pomace brandies into a separate business.

In addition to pomaces from their own twenty hectares (forty-nine acres), they process pressing leftovers from the Piedmont DOC regions Asti, Cuneo, and Alessandra. The actual sources are indicated on the label, and one can find a number of famous Piedmontese names among them—for example, the *cru* Ciabot Mentin of the *barrique* champion Domenico Clerico. After aging in Inox stainless-steel tanks (which can take more than a year even with white grappas) and a brief period in barrels of Slovenian oak, the distillates are bottled in stylish modern flasks: the single-variety grappas Barbera, Brechetto, Cortese di Gavi, Dolcetto, Grignolino, Malvasia, Moscato, Nebbiolo, and Freisa in 50 cl "Futura" bottles, the *cuvée* grappas aged for more than a year in 70 cl Bordeaux bottles. Two Grappa Riservas age for more than a year in oak barrels and ultimately reach the market in 70 cl Bordeaux bottles. The Rovero estate also has a restaurant well known for its kitchen, whose Piedmontese specialties can be enjoyed with the house grappas as digestives or the apple brandy Aquaviva di Mele from the Roveros' own orchards.

Grappa di Barbera

From pomaces of their own Il Milin estate (92 proof, 70 cl).

Ⅰ *An exceptional brandy for grappa lovers; a tart, masculine grappa with musky overtones; extremely pleasant taste with a bittersweet edge.*

Grappa di Moscato

From pomaces from the Caudrina estate of Redento and Romano Dogliotti, famous for their pioneering work with the muscat grape; aged for a year in stainless-steel tanks (90 proof, 70 cl).

Ⅰ *The perfect muscat grappa; refreshing fruit and floral notes—like a late summer farm-stand with sun-ripened oranges. Takes on depth and fruitiness on the palate, and has a long, delicately bitter-chocolate finish. Wonderful.*

Additional Grappas

Single-variety grappas from dolcetto, freisa, gavi, grignolino, malvasia, nebbiolo, and Nebbiolo Riserva. Also the grappa Il Milin.

SCHIAVO

—◦—

Distilleria Guido Schiavo s.n.c.
Via Mazzini, 39
36030 Costabissara, Veneto

*G*iuseppe Schiavo first started distilling pomaces with his portable still in the Vicenza region in 1887, moving from farm to farm. After World War I he settled in Costabissara, where he built a small distillery consisting of a fermentation facility and a single copper alembic. As early as 1960 his son Guido recognized that he could improve quality if he distilled only very fresh pomaces. Instead of giving space to pomace silos he installed a total of nine stills, in order to be able to distill fresh pomaces immediately after delivery during the harvest period from October to Christmas. Today Guido's son Beppe runs the family business, devoting himself mainly to single-variety grappas from the region's rarer varieties.

Grappa Vera di Clinto

A cult grappa from the rare pomaces of the clinto, a phylloxera-resistant variety imported from America in the 1920s, distilled in single batches (86 proof, 50 cl).

A choice brandy. Powerful aroma of nuts, roast substances, and flowers underlaid with fresh grass, with a soft, warm aroma that strikes a harmonious curve from the first sip through the long finish.

SEGNANA

DISTILLERIA SEGNANA DI FRATELLI LUNELLI S.P.A.
VIA DELLA FOSSA, 5/B
38051 BORGO VALSUGANA, TRENTINO

*T*he Lunelli brothers, established producers of still and
sparkling wines in the village, took
over the small family distillery founded by Paolo Segnana in 1982. They
use six pot stills, some heated with
steam, others double-bottomed. They
produce only single-variety grappas
distilled in single batches.

GRAPPA DI MÜLLER-THURGAU

*A winy distillate with very ripe
fruit aromas of bananas and
berries; medium heavy, powerful
body, gentle finish (84 proof, 50 cl).*

GRAPPA DI PINOT NERO

*An elegant brandy with a bou-
quet of nuts, dates, figs, mushrooms; becomes warmer on the
palate, with spice tones and fruit
notes (84 proof, 50 cl).*

Additional Grappa
GRAPPA DI CHARDONNAY

SIBONA

DISTILLERIA DOMENICO SIBONA & C. S.N.C.
VIA ROMA, 10
12040 PIOBESI D'ALBA, PIEDMONT

*O*ne of the oldest distilleries in the Piedmont, which proudly claims that it was the first to be licensed by the state UTIF authorities. Its founder, Domenico Sibona, was considered an eccentric in Piobesi. One of his madnesses was establishing a business in which he distilled rose petals with steam from an old locomotive. Today the house makes grappa in traditional steam-heated pot stills—the locomotive has been retired. Sibona gets all of its pomaces from well-known Piedmont estates.

GRAPPA BAROLO

From nebbiolo pomaces from the commune of Cannubi, in the vicinity of Barolo, aged in oak barrels (88 proof, 50 cl).

An amber-colored distillate with an intense, very spicy aroma and fruit notes both ripe (dried fruit) and fresh (orange, grapefruit, lemons). Winy sweet on the palate, with a warm finish. A real spice package.

Nebbiolo grapes, the "Pearls of the Piedmont"

Grappa Moscato

From muscat pomaces from the commune of Valdililla, aged in acacia barrels (88 proof, 50 cl).

🍷 *A radiant gold brandy with a highly complex aroma, almost startlingly fresh, despite floral and ripe fruit tones. On the palate these really take off, before settling into a delicately bitter finish. An athlete with feeling.*

Additional Grappas

Grappa di Dolcetto, *from dolcetto pomaces from the Bertulot vineyard in the commune of Montelupo d'Alba*

Grappa di Favorita, *from pomaces of the very rare favorita grape from Conegliano, Piobesi, Vezza, and Monteu Roero*

Grappa di Arneis, *from hand-selected pomaces from the communes of Montaldo, Monteu, Vezza, and S. Stefano Roero*

Grappa di Barbaresco, *from nebbiolo pomaces from Neive parish vineyards*

LA TASTEVIN

**DISTILLERIA ASTIGIANA DI FRANCO BARBERO/
LA TASTEVIN SAS
VIA CAVOUR, 6
14047 MOMBERCELLI D'ASTI, PIEDMONT**

A Piedmontese distillery that has specialized in the production of fashionable grappe d'arte and is known for the quality of its products and its original but unexaggerated packaging. The name La Tastevin refers to the old-fashioned copper pot still of the sort once found on every larger wine estate, used for the distillation of pomaces. For the owner of the distillery, Franco Barbero, it symbolizes a synthesis of old traditions and modern distilling. Barbero takes advantage of his distillery's location on the boundary between the Langhe and the Monferrato, two of the Piedmont's main winegrowing regions. The typical vines of the region—muscat, grignolino, barbera, and brachetto—grow in the surrounding vineyards, and the Barbarolo and Barbaresco vineyards are not far away. Short delivery routes and his personal relationships with wine makers guarantee that Barbero secures fresh, moist, first-class pomaces, from which he distills not only single-variety grappas but also mixed brandies typical of the Piedmont.

He uses two large double-bottomed copper stills that stand atop brick stoves, in which La Tastevin brandies have been distilled for more than forty years. Barbero's decades of experience as a distiller are reflected even in his choice of barrels for aging grappa. For his Selezione Oro Legni series he uses homemade barrels of apple, pear, almond, mulberry, juniper, and cherry wood, as well as ash, oak, and acacia. Even his clear brandies are given plenty of time; they all rest for at least a year.

Grappa La Giovane

A clear brandy from fresh Piedmontese pomaces, insofar as possible from the wine-growing communes of Mombercelli, Vaglio, Vinchio, and Montegrosso (86 proof, 75 cl).

A lush grappa with a fresh, distinct aroma of nuts—lightly salted pistachios—and a notable fruit; the round, balanced body sits warmer and winier on the palate.

Grappa Un Amore di Grappa

From moist nebbiolo pomaces and aged in oak (86 proof, 75 cl).

A light gold, somewhat sweet distillate with a harmonious aroma of exotic fruit and lovely secondary aromas: vanilla, caramel, roasted notes; round and full on the palate, with bite in its intense finish.

Additional Grappas

Single varieties Dolcetto d'Alba, Grignolino d'Asti, Nebbiolo da Barolo, Moscato d'Asti, Ruché, Brachetto, and Rossese

Grappa Liberty:
Bianca and Invecchiata

Grappa Ormeasco:
Distillato d'Uva Moscato d'Amburgo, Distillato d'Uva Ruché

TERRE ANTICHE

TERRE ANTICHE DISTILLERIE DELLAVALLE
LOCALITÀ VIGLIANO
14053 ASTI, PIEDMONT

*T*he grappa distiller Roberto Dellavalle considers himself an artist. He calls his three grappas Terre Antiche, or Old Countries, as they are meant to reflect the ancient culinary traditions of his Piedmontese homeland, whose tradition of wine making goes back to the time of the Roman Empire. His distilling method is as traditional as his choice of vines: muscat, nebbiolo da Barolo, and ruché, the native, now very rare vines of the Piedmont. His packaging is artistic: the Greco-Italian artist Carlo Carosso designed labels inspired by classical mythology. Their colors recall the soils of the Asti vineyards—brown sandstone, gray and blue tufa.

Cool morning fog in the Piedmont during autumn

Grappa Barolo

A profound, spicy grappa with dark aroma notes, winy and soft in taste with a lush structure and intense finish (84 proof, 70 cl).

Grappa di Ruché

An opulent brandy with a rich bouquet of spices: vanilla, cinnamon, and candied orange peel; winy sweet on the palate with a long, fruit-dominated finish (84 proof, 70 cl).

Grappa di Moscato Riserva

A tinglingly lively, greenish gold distillate; sumptuous fruit accented with citrus notes, piquant tones of wood (even juniper?) and ripe oranges. Fruity body, with an elegantly bitter finish (84 proof, 70 cl).

TOSOLINI

◦

BEPI TOSOLINI
VIA DELLA ROGGIA, 22
33040 MARSURE DI SOTTO, FRIULI

A small distillery under the direction of the enologist Paolo Tosolini. Instead of grappas, he produces distillates from whole grapes in order to get "products of the greatest individuality and harmony." They come from the DOC growing regions Colli Orientali del Friuli and Grave del Friuli. Gently pressed, the must is fermented with the skins at low temperatures, then distilled with steam in traditional pot stills before alcoholic fermentation is complete and aged in barrels of ash. The barrels serve to harmonize the flavor without altering the color or aroma.

MOST: UVE TIPICO FRIULANE

A blend of such typical Friuli varieties as refosco, ramandolo, and ribolla (86 proof, 70 cl).
A complex but slightly tart brandy with a powerful bouquet in which fresh grassy and floral tones predominate; a substantial, winy taste—like summer in the country.

Additional Grappas
MOST, *from picolit, ribolla, verduzzo di Ramandolo, fragolino, refosco, Müller-Thurgau, pinot grigio, and traminer*

An ancient winepress

VARDA

---◦---

VILLA DE VARDA S.R.L.
VIA E. DE VARDA, 24
38017 MEZZOLOMBARDO, TRENTINO

*A*n estate with a distillery established in the early sixteenth century by the Varda family. Its products were so highly regarded at the court in Vienna that Emperor Leopold I elevated Giovanni de Varda to the nobility in 1678. At the beginning of the nineteenth century Michele Dolzan took over the estate and devoted himself to the scientific study of the art of distilling. The estate continued to enjoy the Hapsburgs' favor; in 1905 Emperor Francis Joseph graciously accepted three bottles of grappa from Giovanni Dolzan distilled solely from teroldego pomaces—one of the first single-variety grappa from the Trentino. Today the distillery produces twelve different single-variety grappas in addition to a blended one. The Italian grappa authority Luigi Veronelli gave his blessing, and the astrologer Lucia Alberti assigned to each grappa its appropriate constellation. Il Caratteri was the result, a grappa zodiac in bottles of delicate Murano glass. Varda also produces fruit distillates, liqueurs, and wine.

Grappa Classica Trentina

*From a mix of Trentino pomaces in a limited edition of 9,842
bottles, distilled in single batches in a double-bottomed pot still
(80 proof, 70 cl).*

🍷 *Our sample no. 4,160: Harmonious and lovely, with a tropical fruit bouquet (oranges, peaches, apricots, bananas,
pineapple); winy in taste, with a reserved sweetness and a long
finish.*

Additional Grappas

Collezione Caratteri: *Grappa Pinot Grigio (Aries);
Sauvignon (Taurus), Merlot (Gemini), Müller-
Thurgau (Cancer), Teroldego (Leo), Lagrein
(Virgo), Moscato (Libra), Cabernet (Scorpio),
Marzemino (Sagittarius), Pinot Nero (Capricorn),
Chardonnay (Aquarius), and Schiava (Pisces)*

Collezione Mormorio della Foresta:
*Four single-variety grappas from chardonnay,
merlot, muscat, and teroldego and the Grappa
Mormorio Riserva, aged in barrels*

Collezione Chiar di Luna: *Four
single-variety grappas from Müller-Thurgau,
marzemino, cabernet, and schiava*

Grappa Mattino Teroldego

VILLANOVA

DISTILLERIA VAL DI ROSE DI TENUTA VILLANOVA
VIA CONTESSA BERETTA, 7
34070 FARRA D'ISONZO, FRIULI

A small distillery attached to the Villanova estate, established in 1499 in the Collio hills of the Friuli. Grapes are grown on the estate specifically for distilling and harvested early to preserve their strong acid and lend greater character to the brandy. The operation employs both steam and double-bottomed stills, distilling in single batches.

VAL DI ROSE TRAMINER (1991)

Distilled in a limited edition of 2,361 bottles (90 proof, 70 cl).

Our sample no. 228: A round but fresh and fruity brandy, soft on the palate, with deep, ripe tones and a tart sweetness; a thoroughbred traminer distillate.

MONTE CUCCO CABERNET

(90 proof, 50 cl)

A highly aromatic brandy, winy and nutty in aroma, with a powerful development in flavor from sweet to bitter.

Harvesting in Friuli

Additional Grappas

———◦———

*I*n addition to those presented in this book, there are of course many more grappas from well-known wine makers and distilleries on the market. We are forever coming across new pomace brandies from reputable houses. Unfortunately, there is not enough room in this book to discuss them all, yet these high-class brandies should not go unmentioned.

ABBAZIA DI NOVACELLA *(Alto Adige)*

SÈREGO ALIGHIERE *(Veneto)*

ALLEGRINI *(Veneto)*

ELIO ALTARE *(Piedmont)*

ANTONIO ANGELI *(Trentino)*

ANTONIOLO *(Piedmont)*

AZELIA *(Piedmont)*

ERIK BANTI *(Tuscany)*

BARALE *(Piedmont)*

BAVA *(Piedmont)*

FRATELLI BERA *(Piedmont)*

BORGO SANTO *(Veneto)*

BOSCO DEL MERLO *(Veneto)*

BOSSO *(Piedmont)*

BROGLIA *(Piedmont)*

LA CALONICA *(Tuscany)*

CANTALUPO *(Piedmont)*

CAPANNA *(Tuscany)*

CAPEZZANA *(Tuscany)*

CASANUOVA DELLE CERBAIE *(Tuscany)*

LE CASE BIANCHE *(Veneto)*

CASETTA DEI FRATI *(Piedmont)*

CASINA DI CORNIA *(Tuscany)*

CASTELGIOCONDO *(Tuscany)*

CASTELLARE DI CASTELLINA *(Tuscany)*

CASTELLO DI AMA *(Tuscany)*

CASTELLO DI LIGNANO *(Piedmont)*

CASTELLO DI NEIVE *(Piedmont)*

CASTELLO DI QUERCETO *(Tuscany)*

CASTELLO DI UZZANO *(Tuscany)*

CAUDRINA *(Piedmont)*

CENNATOIO *(Tuscany)*

FLAVIO COMAR *(Friuli)*

CONCILIO *(Trentino)*

IL CONVENTINO *(Tuscany)*

JUIGI COPPO *(Piedmont)*

AZIENDA DEI *(Tuscany)*

FARNETA *(Tuscany)*

FRATELLI FASOLI *(Veneto)*

FULIGNI *(Tuscany)*

GIOVI *(Sicily)*

MARCHESE INCISA *(Tuscany)*

CANTINE ISOLA *(Sardinia)*

LA LECCIAIA *(Tuscany)*

LETRARI *(Trentino)*

LIBRANDI *(Calabria)*

MADONNA DELLE VITTORIE *(Trentino)*

MARCATI *(Veneto)*

MARCHESI DI BAROLO *(Piedmont)*

MARZADRO *(Trentino)*

MASO CANTANGHEL *(Trentino)*

MASO ROVERI *(Trentino)*

FILIPPO MAZZETTI *(Piedmont)*

LUIGI MINUTO *(Piedmont)*

MONTE VERTINE *(Tuscany)*

MUSSO *(Piedmont)*

GIOACCHINO NANNONI *(Tuscany)*

NOTTOLA *(Tuscany)*

NUOVA CAPPELLATTA *(Piedmont)*

PASOLINI *(Lombardy)*

PETRETO *(Tuscany)*

PIRCHER *(Alto Adige)*

POGGIOLUNGA *(Tuscany)*

FRANCESCO POLI *(Trentino)*

GIOVANNI POLI *(Trentino)*

PRAVIS *(Trentino)*

PRODUTTORI DI CORMÒNS *(Friuli)*

PSENNER *(Alto Adige)*

PUNSET DIE MARCARINO *(Tuscany)*

LE RAGOSE *(Veneto)*

RIPARBELLO *(Tuscany)*

ROCCA DELLE MACIE *(Tuscany)*

ROCHE *(Piedmont)*

ROSA DEL GOLFO
(Apulia)

ROSSO *(Piedmont)*

LE SALETTE *(Veneto)*

SAN FELICE *(Tuscany)*

SAN LEONARDO *(Trentino)*

SANTA BARBARA
(The Marches)

SAVIGNOLA *(Tuscany)*

ANTONIO SCAMBIA
(Umbria)

CONTI SERTOLI SALIS
(Lombardy)

PRINCIPE STROZZI
(Tuscany)

CANTINA DEL TABURNO
(Campania)

DE TARCZAL *(Trentino)*

TRANQUILLINI *(Trentino)*

UNTERTHURNER
(Alto Adige)

VALDIPIATTA *(Tuscany)*

VAL DI SUGA *(Tuscany)*

VIGNANO *(Tuscany)*

VILLA COLONNA
(Tuscany)

VILLA MATILDE
(Campania)

VILLA SCERIMAN *(Veneto)*

LA VOLTA *(Piedmont)*

ZANIN *(Veneto)*

GAETANO ZENI *(Veneto)*

Enjoying Grappa

⟶◦▶⟶

One can, of course, take a sip of grappa for breakfast, as it is said that the Italians do—though our own observations suggest that this is only a vicious rumor. But certainly grappa serves as the perfect digestive, a harmonious conclusion to a meal, especially if wine has been served. If it was an Italian meal and an Italian wine, so much the better. Moreover, if the grappa is matched to the wine—that is, if they are both from the same grape variety—the experience is true perfection.

To be sure, the grappa must be served at the proper temperature. For young and delicate grappas this should be between 46 and 50 degrees Fahrenheit (8 and 10 degrees C), whereas an older grappa aged in the barrel is most enjoyable at between 61 and 64 degrees Fahrenheit (16 and 18 degrees C). Even the most careful chilling is wasted if one serves the grappa in small brandy glasses—especially chilled ones, as the host at the corner pizzeria used to do. The queen of wine spirits is a fragile creature whose aroma needs to be brought to full bloom—no one would dream of presenting a noble cognac or malt whisky in a tumbler.

THE RIGHT GLASS

It is becoming widely recognized that no glass can turn a bad brandy into a good one, but it can certainly allow a complex distillate to show off all its facets.

Harald L. Bremer, an engineer and wine dealer from Brunswick, Germany, was the first to create an appropriately elegant glass for grappa: delicate, long-stemmed, made of hand-blown lead crystal. The thin walls of the upper part of the glass made it possible, for the first time, to appreciate fully nuances of

Grappa glass from
Spiegelau's Grand
Palais series

Bremer's grappa glass

Grappa glass from
Riedel's Sommelier series

Grappa glass from Schott-Zwiesel's
Domaine line

the aroma. Broad at the base, the glass narrows to a straight chimney in which alcohol and aroma are balanced before coming into contact with the nose. Bremer, represented in this guide as a grappa-producing wine maker himself (see San Michele), was particularly concerned with everyday practicality: his delicate glasses are dishwasher proof and can even withstand rough treatment in restaurants.

Durability was also a concern for the well-known glassmakers Schott-Zwiesel and Riedel, who have sought to produce professional glasses that would also appeal to individuals. Two variants are offered by Schott: the grappa glass in the Domaine line was created by the designer Alois Drexler; the one from the Sélection line comes from the Zwiesel studio. The cult glassmaker Riedel, in Kufstein, Germany, added to its Sommelier series a grappa glass with a slender chalice shape.

After seeking the advice of experienced sommeliers, the crystal producer Spiegelau came out with the Grand Palais series, in collaboration with wine stewards and wine makers. These hand-blown glasses are carefully structured, with a slender, graceful tulip shape instead of a wide chalice. Advantage: the minimal surface for evaporation concentrates the aromas and provides for a harmonious blend of alcoholic bite and fragrance. Another crucial point for the designer was minimizing the risk of breakage. Fire-polished edges were the solution—with that technique the glass loses tension, gains elasticity, and is dishwasher proof.

Special grappa glasses are now available in almost every price range. However, those who have run out of space in their cupboards can console themselves with the fact that both young and aged grappas are perfectly enjoyable when served in a simple "nosing glass" of the sort originated by cognac distillers for blending their cognac *cuvée* and now used by master distillers and tasters for almost all the available digestives. If you don't have those, and don't want to spend a fortune acquiring them, sherry glasses come close in shape and function to the glasses generally used for spirits.

Cooking with Grappa

Grappa is scarcely mentioned in the classic Italian cookbooks, but it certainly finds its uses in the Italian kitchen. Italian housewives are fond of adding a dash of grappa for flavor—not an expensive, noble grappa but a simple one in a thick-walled, everyday bottle. The cuisine of the north, with its strong, intense flavors, especially values the spicy aroma of grappa, which enhances the character of rustic specialties and obediently adapts to the changing seasons. From New Year's Day to Christmas, the Italians find endless ways of using grappa.

In the Friuli, whose cuisine reflects the cooking of Austria and the Balkans, a New Year's eve or New Year's morning tradition is the *pinza*, a yeast cake with either a sweet or savory filling, flambéed with grappa to drive away evil spirits. Venice's famous *dolce di Carnevale*, a richly decorated chocolate torte, is filled with an egg cream frequently flavored with grappa. Once Carnival is past, people in the Veneto and in Liguria turn their attention to the noblest of Lenten fare: fresh fish from the sea—served cold as an appetizer, marinated in a mixture of lemon juice and grappa; or grilled, drizzled with a little grappa . . .

After Easter the first fruits and vegetables begin to ripen. Despite freezers and hothouses, people still put up their own produce in Italy: grappa adds zest to marmalades as well as to pickled vegetables. It spices the *peperonata* and fruit salad; gives flavor to the Ligurian *zabaione secco*, in which fresh vegetables are dipped; and with the addition of a little mint is used to marinate shrimp salad with homemade mayonnaise, for which there are countless variant recipes on the Italian Riviera. Grappa intensifies Genoa's pesto, gives a piquant touch to antipasti heavy with the scent of olive oil, and soothes the palate as a sorbet after a summer menu. The South also has its uses for grappa. A light brushing of grappa on either Neapolitan pizza or the *bruschetta* from Apulia intensifies the flavor of the warm bread and the scent of herbs. Even *sete*, a dessert made of pomegranates, is frequently flavored with grappa.

You can also smell the aromas of grappa wherever cheese is made in Emilia-Romagna or the Piedmont. Various local specialty cheeses are regularly brushed with grappa. It is also used to flavor the local fondue, a thick mixture of melted Fontina cheese from the Val d'Aosta, milk, and egg yolk. In the fall, when the grapes are being harvested and grappa is distilled, the Piedmontese wine maker's wife is likely to serve a dip for vegetables and breadsticks called *bagna calda,* made of garlic, oil, and anchovies and made more digestible with a dash of grappa. In the Alto Adige, farmers get out their stills and invite their friends to a distilling bash. They either slaughter a pig or order sausages and ribs from the butcher, then cook them in the lid of the still in the hot steam from the pomace. It gives the grappa a rustic aroma and a delightful flavor to the meat. When making homemade salami and sausages they always add a healthy shot of grappa. In hunting season, grappa is traditionally added to strong sauces for wild game, to cranberries, or to marinades for venison goulashes. As Christmas approaches, the Italians set about their baking. The Lombard *panettone,* also popular in Tuscany, is drenched with grappa. At Florian's, the oldest café in Venice, *biscotti* are served with pear grappa. And the housewife perfumes her Christmas cookies and cakes with the brandy most likely to be at hand at hand—grappa.

MIXING WITH GRAPPA

Grappa lovers rarely find their favorite brandy mixed in classic bar drinks. Bartenders are likely to explain: "It used to be that grappa was unknown, and now good grappas are too expensive to use." This is an argument that the producers of brand-name grappas refuse to accept. Intensely flavored and decoratively but not expensively packaged, their products offer quality for the price. Thanks to the efforts of the large distilleries, the Society of Grappa Tasters, and the Italian branch of the International Bartenders Association, in recent years there has been a veritable flood of newly created cocktails with grappa. But neither the

Sunrise in the Alps, the Sunset over Cernobbio, the Miramare, nor La Grotta has been able to gain popularity. Headstrong diva that she is, grappa is not about to share the stage with Campari, Cointreau, and company. But she is certainly not above putting in an appearance in the classic cocktails.

Consider the Sour, for example, the standby cocktail of the 1930s:

Grappa Sour

4–6 tsp. (2–3 cl) lemon juice
2–4 tsp. (1–2 cl) sugar syrup
3 tbsp. plus 1 tsp. (5 cl) grappa
Stir with ice

If you top it off with soda, the Grappa Sour becomes a Livia Collins, the Italian sister of Tom Collins (juice, syrup, and soda with gin), Pedro Collins (with rum), Sandy Collins (with Scotch), or Pepito Collins (with tequila).

If the trio of juice, syrup, and alcohol is shaken, not stirred, and topped with soda, you have a Grappa Fizz.

Also delightful is a grappa highball—grappa on ice with soda, a dash of orange bitters, and garnished with a lemon peel. This is especially good with a grappa di moscato.

Grappa makes an elegant julep, a cocktail that Scarlett O'Hara might have savored. For a Grappa Julep, crush fresh mint leaves in a mortar with sugar, add them to 2 tbsp. plus 2 tsp. (4 cl) grappa, fill the glass up to the edge with crushed ice, and decorate with a sprig of mint.

Needless to say, grappa is a natural with coffee. The Caffè Corretto—hot espresso with a shot of grappa—is an Italian national drink. But you owe it to yourself to try cold coffee with grappa: allow first-class espresso with plenty of sugar to cool, stir in 4 tsp. (2 cl) grappa, and sprinkle with cloves and cinnamon—a true pick-me-up.

And what would be more obvious than topping a prosecco grappa with Prosecco Spumante and a dash of grapefruit juice?

Given its distinctive flavor, grappa can serve as an interesting base for classic cocktail recipes, and it should also inspire experimentation and discovery.

Grappa on the Internet

———◦———

*M*ore and more information about grappa can be found on the Internet. Even though most Web pages related to grappa are in Italian, this is a useful trend nonetheless. The Centro Studi e Formazione Assaggiatori, which houses the Istituto Nazionale Grappa, provides a lot of information, and its site is constantly being expanded. A number of grappa importers and dealers also include background information about their products on their home pages. It is worthwhile to browse the Web for new information on a regular basis.

GENERAL ADDRESSES

The Centro Studi e Formazione Assaggiatori can be reached at http://www.terradimare.com/assaggiatore.htm. The site also offers an archive with articles, in Italian, on the current state of grappa. The same organization provides information on another Web site, where you can read *Grappa News* (again, only in Italian). The most current issue can be seen at http://tdm.dmw.it/grappanews.htm, which also provides a link to an archive of back issues.

PRODUCERS' HOME PAGES

Some of the producers discussed in this book have home pages on the Internet or are described in detail on pages dealing with their region:

www.avignonesi.it/grappa-vs.htm
Information on the grappas from the Avignonesi winery

www.domenis.it
Distilleria Emilio Domenis

www.inga.it
Distillerie Inga

www.mangilli.com
Mangilli distillery

www.marchesidigresy.com
Marchesi di Gresy winery

www.pojeresandri.it
The winemakers and distillers Pojer & Sandri

www.trentinodoc.it/pisoni/
The winemakers and distillers Pisoni

Importers

———◦———

*I*n the last few years, grappas have become available in increasing variety even in smaller liquor stores. And if there's a grappa you want to try that's not on the shelf, many stores will special order it for you. The importers listed below supply grappas to distributors, who in turn sell them to local stores. They may be able to tell you what shop in your vicinity carries the brand you're looking for.

BANFI VINTNERS
1111 Cedar Swamp Road
Old Brookville, New York 11545
Phone: (516) 626-9200
Fax: (516) 626-9218
Specializes in Castello Banfi grappas

CLICQUOT, INC.
717 Fifth Avenue
New York, New York 10022
Phone: (212) 888-7575
Fax: (212) 888-7551
Specializes in Ceretto and Capezzana grappas

LAIRD & COMPANY
One Laird Road
Scobeyville, New Jersey 07724
Phone: (732) 542-0312
Fax: (732) 542-2244
Specializes in Mazetti d'Altavilla grappas

PATERNO IMPORTS
900 Armour Drive
Lake Bluff, Illinois 60044
Phone: (847) 604-8900
Fax: (847) 604-5828

Beth Petrovich
NONINO

TYFIELD IMPORTS
1410 Allen Drive
Troy, Michigan 48083
Phone: (248) 589-8282
Fax: (248) 589-2655
Specializes in Varda grappas NO

la Marca
chard
Pinot grigio
Elaine Annese
EANNESE@Viniferainports.com

VINIFERA IMPORTS
205 13th Avenue
Ronkonkoma, New York 11779
Phone: (631) 467-5907
Fax: (631) 467-6516
Specializes in Castello di Barbaresco, Felsina, and Gaja grappas

WINEBOW, INC.
22 Hollywood Avenue, Suite C
Hohokus, New Jersey 07423
Phone: (201) 445-0620
Fax: (201) 445-9869
Specializes in Badia a Coltibuono, Nardini, Jacopo Poli, and Zenato grappas

8X 416 Lina handles Badia & Zenato
Camarota

Glossary

———◦►———

ACQUAVITE D'UVA: A distillate made from whole fermented grapes, rather than from pomace.

BARRIQUE: Small barrels made of French oak, used to age wine and brandies.

CONTINUOUS DISTILLATION: Mass-production method of distillation in which large batches of pomace are steamed "continuously" in gigantic cauldrons.

CUVÉE: Blend of pomaces from different grape varieties.

DISCONTINUOUS DISTILLATION: Traditional method of distillation, in which small batches of pomace are heated in a copper still, which is cleaned and refilled after each distillation. This process yields more aromatic and intense grappas than continuous distillation.

DISTALLATA A BAGNOMARIA (distilled in a water bath): This term on a label indicates that a grappa has been produced in a double-bottomed pot still, which distributes heat more evenly and results in a higher-quality grappa.

DISTILLATA A VAPORE (distilled in steam): This term on a label indicates that a grappa has been produced in a steam alembic, or still, which also results in a higher-quality grappa.

DOC (DENOMINAZIONE DI ORIGINE CONTROLLATA): This term on a label indicates that a wine originated in a specific geographic zone and met the quality requirements specified by Italy's system of wine regulation, established in 1963.

DOCG (DENOMINAZIONE DI ORIGINE CONTROLLATA E GARANTITA): This term on a label indicates that a wine has "guaranteed authenticity," an indication of even higher quality within a DOC.

FUSEL OIL: An oily liquid, with a disagreeable color and taste, found in insufficiently distilled alcohols.

GRAPPA: A brandy made only in Italy, distilled from pomace according to strict regulations and aged a minimum of six months.

HARMONIZE: The process of maturing the fresh distillate in glass or steel tanks, or in casks, in order to balance the components that produce the spirit's aroma.

INVECCHIATA (aged), STRAVECCHIA (very old), or riserva (reserve): A label may use these terms to indicate that a grappa has been aged more than the legal minimum of six months.

MARC: Both a synonym for pomace and the generic name for the brandy made from that residue. This term on a label indicates the maturation of the pomace in wooden casks.

MUST: The nonfermented juice extracted from grapes during the pressing.

POMACE: The residue of skins, seeds, and so on left after grapes are crushed for wine.

RACKING: During fermentation this process is used to siphon the liquid off the thick deposit of yeast and solids.

SPRITZIG: A fizzy, almost effervescent quality in young and acidic white wines.

Index

———◦———

Vintners and distillers appear in **boldface;** specific grappas are in regular type.